THE
BRICKTIONARY
The ultimate LEGO® A–Z

RYAN McNAUGHT

murdoch books

Sydney | London

Contents

Hi there,

I'm Ryan. Everyone knows me as 'Brickman': I'm a LEGO® Certified Professional, one of a select few in the world and the only one in the Southern Hemisphere. It's my job to make cool and incredible LEGO models for lots of stores and events around the world.

I'm lucky enough to also be the judge on *LEGO Masters Australia*, where I get to see all manner of brilliant LEGO creations. One thing that never ceases to amaze me on the show is the creativity and imagination that the contestants have: it really does know no bounds!

I am always being asked, 'Where does all this LEGO knowledge and skill come from? How do you know so much about LEGO?' That's when it struck me: why not make a book that tries to explain everything we know about LEGO? Then take that even further (because we love a challenge) and use that knowledge to throw out some ideas that will help spark your imagination as well.

And so *The Bricktionary* was born: an A to Z of LEGO ideas you can use in infinite ways. There are cool design challenges to inspire you, tips on techniques to improve your skills and definitions of LEGO words so you can talk like a pro.

There is nothing more satisfying in the LEGO world than not only coming up with an amazing idea, but also executing that idea into an incredible LEGO model. *The Bricktionary* will show you how.

I can't wait to see what you come up with, and where your creativity and new skills take you.

RYAN McNAUGHT
LEGO® CERTIFIED PROFESSIONAL

How to use this book

The Bricktionary is designed to be used any way you like: you can dive right in at your favourite letter; open a page at random to see what turns up; start from the beginning and work your way through – or you can even read it backwards! No matter how you do it, the ideas will come to you. From A to Z, each letter is packed with inspiration for ingenious builds and insider tips and tricks to take your LEGO® skills to the next level. Plus, you don't need an army of family and friends to make incredible creations. The ideas in this book can be used to build things on your own, or with others – it's up to you. Here's what's inside:

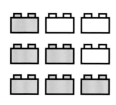

A–Z OF DESIGN CHALLENGES

Ideas to spark your imagination – everything from an Action Figure to a Zebra! They are rated Basic (1 brick), Intermediate (2 bricks) or Advanced (3 bricks), but don't be afraid to step outside your comfort zone.

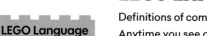

LEGO LANGUAGE

Definitions of commonly used words in the LEGO world. Anytime you see a word highlighted **like this**, you'll find the definition in alphabetical order by the first letter.

PRO TECHNIQUES

Expert tips that will help show you the different ways that LEGO can be used to make all the things you want to build.

What LEGO bricks do I need?

The great thing about this book is that you don't need a particular LEGO set, or a specific type of LEGO. LEGO bricks are so versatile, they can literally be anything. The only thing you need to get the most out of your bricks is your imagination. Sometimes we talk about particular LEGO parts: it's not a problem if you don't have that exact part, as often you can solve the problem in many different ways. Remember, it's not how much LEGO you have, but how you use it!

There is no right or wrong

With LEGO, there is no such thing as a right or wrong answer: there are just millions, or billions – in fact, bazillions – of potential ways you can achieve something. Imagine you are building your first spaceship: it has awesome wings, but while you are building it you think of all of the other things you should add. It needs an astronaut kitchen, a lunar lander . . . the list goes on. The next time you build a spaceship it will be grander and full of so many more incredible stories!

Failure is A-OK in our LEGO brick world

You know what totally rocks in LEGO? Failure. Sounds strange doesn't it? Imagine this: you build a bridge, but the poor LEGO car that crosses that bridge doesn't make it and falls off down into the LEGO crocodile-infested waters. That's perfectly OK – the LEGO minifigures will miraculously survive – and the next time you build that bridge, you know not to make the same failure point. That's the joy of LEGO: you get free, unlimited do-overs!

The key here is a sometimes overused word: learning. The super-cool thing about LEGO is that you're learning all the time, and you don't even know it.

TRY THE LEGO GUESSING GAME

Look at the models on the opening page for each letter. How many can you identify? See page 349 for the answers.

A is for...

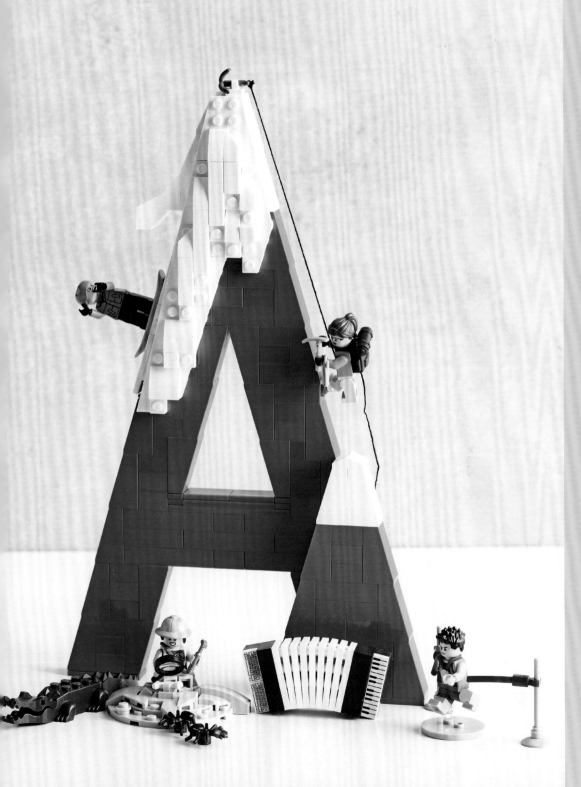

ACTION FIGURE

Action figures are lots of fun to play with, and with LEGO® you can make any person you wish. There are lots of ball-and-socket **joints** you can use to make posable characters, and you can add any special actions you want with simple LEGO **Technic**™ mechanisms; for example, holding and strumming an instrument, an egg-flipping action, or a flying karate chop. Make a model of your uncle doing a funny dance, or a superhero with lasers for eyes: you could use light bricks (see page 167). What about a character from a book you love? Or maybe you have a special person in your life whom you consider a hero? Try to make an action figure that not only looks like the character, but consider giving it a fun action as well.

TRY THIS!

- [ ] How many joints? Remember, if its hips can move, its ankles should as well.
- [ ] Give the figure something to hold.
- [ ] Two or more action figures can create a scene, such as a battle or a dance-off.

ADDITION

Take a broken or incomplete thing and add to it with LEGO. Use the LEGO to enhance it, fix it, support it, or make it complete. Now there are no excuses for why that broken cupboard handle can't be fixed, or the desk organised with a LEGO pencil holder and paper tray. How about a decorative pot for a poor old houseplant that needs livening up, or a vibrato arm for an electric guitar? The possibilities are endless.

TRY THIS!

☐ Match the original colours, or make the additions colourful!
☐ Make the fix tell a story about why the object is broken.

LEGO Language

Accessory
(noun) *say* uhk-sesuhree

Additional **parts** to add to **minifigures**, including bodywear, headgear, handheld items, hairpieces weapons, and much more. Every minifigure should have the right accessories.

AFOL
(noun) *say* ay-fol

Acronym for Adult Fan Of LEGO. Usage: 'Many AFOLs like to use **Travis bricks**.' *See also* **KFOL** and **YFOL**.

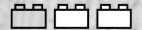

ADVENT CALENDAR

Celebrate the countdown to a special day, such as a birthday, anniversary or holiday, by making a secret model for each day leading up to the event. Each build should be related to the special occasion in some way. Hide the builds in a box with doors for each different day.

TRY THIS!

- [ ] Try to theme the box and doors to the event. If it's your birthday, you could use your favourite colours.
- [ ] Use printed **tiles** or LEGO **parts** to add numbers to the doors.

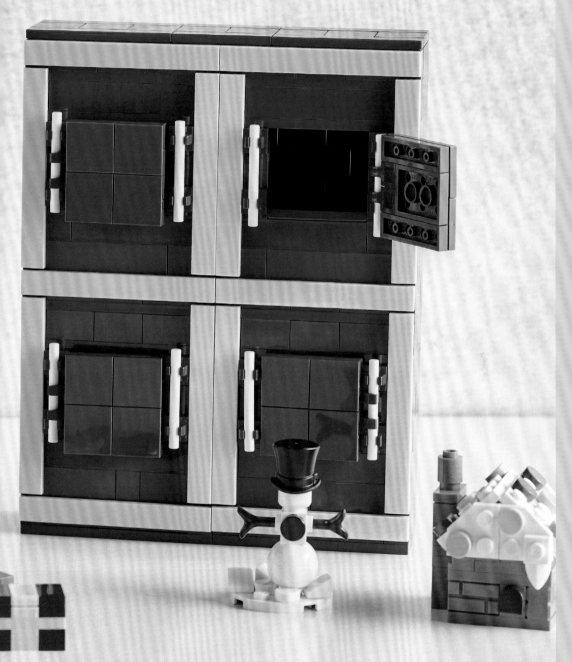

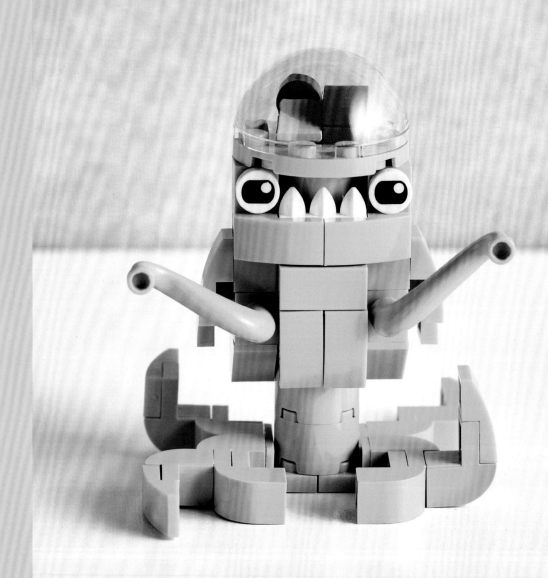

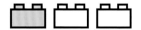

ALIEN

There's a lot of life here on Earth, from plants, fish, birds, mammals and bugs, all the way up to humans. We've adapted to life in our environment, but what do you think aliens from other planets would look like, especially if the conditions on their planet were different to ours? Would they have webbed feet, or giant eyes, or a see-through skull? Build a creature from a planet that is different to Earth.

TRY THIS!

☐ Look to Earth's creatures for inspiration, but add a weird twist.
☐ Building something Alien is a great opportunity for some **N.P.U.** See if you can experiment with some unusual LEGO pieces.

LEGO Language

Antenna
(noun) *say* antenuh

Any long, thin LEGO piece that has an **anti-stud connection** at one end and can be used as an antenna. Usually a **bar-**sized thickness that can be held by a **minifigure**.

Anti-stud
(noun) *say* antee-stud

The inset area, usually at the bottom of a LEGO piece, that will grip and hold a **stud** to make a **connection**. Also called a clutch or a grip. They are not opposed to the idea of studs; they are just a space for the stud to be.

ANIMATION

Make your own videos by taking photos of LEGO models and **minifigures**, moving them slightly, bit by bit, for each new picture. Use a camera or your phone, holding it steady and making sure it's in the same position each time, so that when you put the photos together (there are free apps you can download to help with this) and play them back at speed, you can see your animation in motion. You could even make a camera stand out of LEGO!

TRY THIS!

☐ Use clear parts, such as **antennas**, to hold minifigs in mid-air.
☐ Watch real videos in slow motion to work out how to position your characters and models.

LEGO Language

Arch
(noun) *say* ahch

A **brick** with a curved section removed from it, primarily used to create architectural features. They are good for making space in a wall for **minifigures** to walk through, because without them they'll just get a sore head.

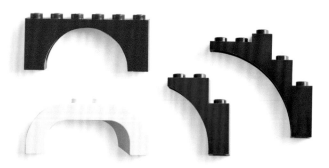

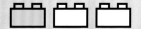

ART

Show your artistic side and create a LEGO picture to display in your house. You can use large pieces to make the shapes in the picture, or you can use small pieces to create a mosaic effect.

TRY THIS!

- [ ] Copy famous artworks.
- [ ] Abstract art is cool.
- [ ] Add a frame to your art.

MONA LISA BY LEONARDO DA VINCI

PRO TECHNIQUE
ANGLES

Some of the trickiest structures to build with LEGO are odd angles for strangely shaped objects, such as roofs and diagonal walls. There are some simple techniques you can use to make angled sections easier to create and work with. **Hinges**, **clips** and **bars**, ball **joints** for pivoting **bricks** and **plates**, and **wedge** plates are all great ways of getting the shapes and angles you need in your builds.

WEDGE PLATES

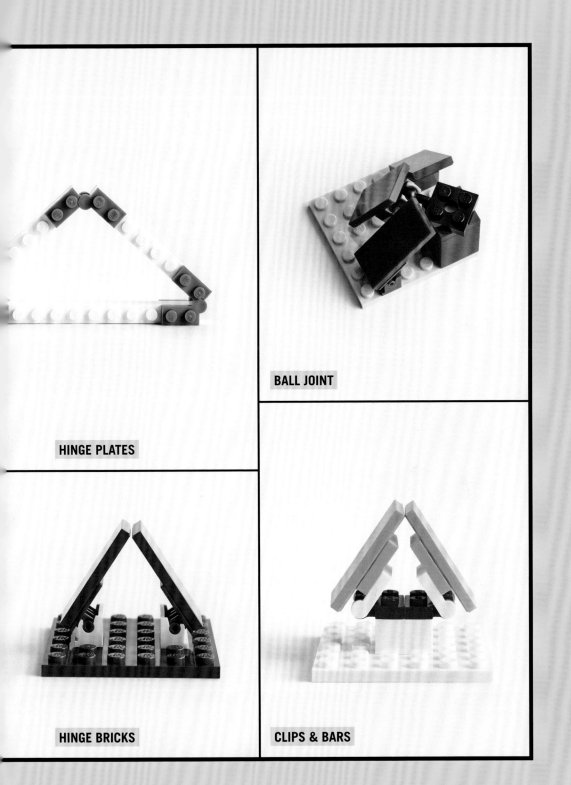

BALL JOINT

HINGE PLATES

HINGE BRICKS

CLIPS & BARS

B is for...

B

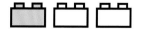

BATH TOY

When LEGO® **bricks** are put together, they trap air inside, so they float on water. Use LEGO to make bath toys, such as a tugboat, a frog, a cruise liner or a cupholder. Press the bricks together firmly to trap the air. You've heard of **swooshable** – well, this is **splooshable**.

TRY THIS!

- [ ] How big can you build something before it sinks?
- [ ] Make sure your build is stable in the water, so it won't capsize.

LEGO Language

Bar
(noun) *say* bah

A bar refers to a long, thin, stick-like piece that can be gripped by a **minifigure** hand or a **clip**. Sometimes bars are moulded into other **parts**, such as **plates** or **bricks**, to allow more **connections**. Quite often bars are used in utensils and weapons so that they can be held by a minifigure. *Also known as*: wand, pole.

Baseplate
(noun) *say* baysplayt

A large, slightly flexible LEGO **plate** used for larger constructions. Thinner than a regular LEGO plate, the baseplate doesn't usually have **anti-studs** on the underside. A baseplate is a good base on which to build a house, a building or an evil … base.

BIRDHOUSE

If you have lots of birdlife in your yard or in nearby trees, you could make a nice birdhouse out of LEGO. Make it big enough for the birds to feed or nest inside, sheltered from the elements, and place it somewhere outside. If there aren't many birds in your area, you could use your imagination and create an ornamental birdhouse and a LEGO bird to go with it.

TRY THIS!

☐ Use LEGO **Technic**™ to strengthen the post and frame.

LEGO Language

Bley
(adjective) *say* blay

A portmanteau that combines 'blue' and 'grey' to describe a shade of LEGO **brick** that is officially called 'Stone Grey'. The old LEGO grey colour had a yellowish hue, and the new one is a bluish-grey colour. Usage: 'I only have that piece in Bley, not grey.'

New Bley brick   **Old grey brick**

BOLOCs
(noun) *say* boluhks

Acronym for Build Of Lots Of Colours. Refers to a build that doesn't pay attention to grouping or arranging the different colours of **bricks** in any way, leading to a build with random bricks and colours.

BOOKENDS

Use your imagination to create a set of themed bookends to prop up your books. They could depict characters and events from your favourite stories, and be as simple or as detailed as you wish.

TRY THIS!

☐ Try to theme the bookends to tell their own story, with one being the start and one being the end.
☐ Make one end the hero, and the other the villains.
☐ Books are heavy: strengthen the vertical section.

Let's hope this London Bridge doesn't fall down!

BRIDGE

Build a bridge: you could copy an actual bridge, such as London Bridge or the Sydney Harbour Bridge, or you could build one across a gap between pieces of furniture. It could be a footbridge for **minifigures** or a traffic bridge for LEGO cars in your LEGO town. If you want a difficult challenge, try to span a large gap.

TRY THIS!

- [ ] Make a **microscale** bridge between objects on your desk.
- [ ] How long can you make your bridge without it falling down?

LEGO Language

Bracket
(noun) *say* brakuht

A bracket is a LEGO plate that has a thinner, perpendicular piece attached to its side. The bracket is either above or below the plate level and comes in various sizes. Brackets are good for making **SNOT** builds (see pages 258–259). Want something hanging off the side of your build? The bracket is your friend.

Brick
(noun) *say* brik

Invented in 1958 by Ole Kirk Kristiansen, a LEGO brick is a small plastic interlocking building brick approximately 1 cm (⅜ inch) in height and of various widths, lengths and colours. The most recognisable is a 'two by four' (2x4): two **studs** by four studs (below right).

Brick-built
(adjective) *say* brik-bilt

Any model or section of a model that is created from regular LEGO **bricks** and **plates** without using any special pieces of any other kind. Literally: built from bricks.

Brick-height
(adjective) *say* brik-huyt

The equivalent of the height of a LEGO **brick**, about 1 cm (⅜ inch). If a **part** is the same height as a brick without being a brick, it's referred to as being 'brick-height'. If you stack three **plates** on top of each other, they are equal to one brick height.

Broomability
(adjective) *say* broom ['oo' as in 'good']-uh'biluhtee

An evaluation of how well a model can be picked up and moved around on a surface to simulate driving ('broom'). A small, sturdy buggy has high broomability, whereas an ostrich has low broomability. *See also* **swooshability** and **splooshability**.

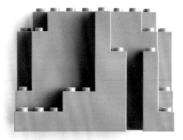

BURP
(noun) *say* berp

BURP is an acronym for Big Ugly Rock Piece and refers to large LEGO pieces moulded with a rough, jagged appearance to represent rocky surfaces. BURPs replace what would be more complex, brick-heavy builds. *See also* **LURP**.

Bugs

Bugs come in so many colours, shapes and sizes that they are perfect for building in LEGO. Bugs have lots of legs, so work out how many you want your bug to have and start building lots of them. You don't need to use all the fancy LEGO ball-joint pieces if you don't have them; you can use **clips** and **bars** or even just use **studs** as **hinges**. Insects are often very colourful, so make sure to decorate your bug with some bright colours in spots or stripes. You can try to build a real-life bug, or make up your own crazy one.

PRO TECHNIQUE
BALANCE

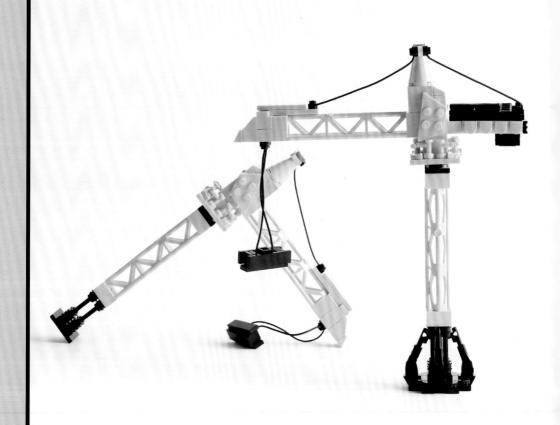

MAKE SURE WEIGHT IS EVENLY DISTRIBUTED

There are two key aspects of balancing your builds. The first is to ensure that your build will be able to stand up and balance by itself. This may mean that you need to add weight to one side so it balances the other, or a stronger support to the base to hold it upright. Start with a wider base, and reinforce supports with LEGO **Technic** or by using **brackets** that span the vertical **bricks** and stop them from toppling over. Refine the structure of your models so they are steady.

The second aspect is balancing the design of your model: there should be balance in the colours and detail. You should ensure that there are no sections of your build that stand out as being too bare or too busy when compared to the rest of the build. Also, think about whether there are any sections of colour that are confined to one area and would be better spread throughout the model. Refine the look of your models so they are pleasing to the eye.

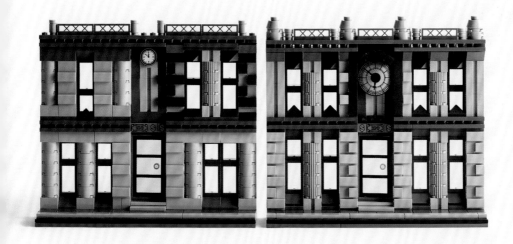

AIM FOR A BALANCED DESIGN

C is for...

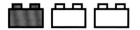

CACTUS

Make a LEGO® cactus. Use any green **bricks** you have for the cactus and don't forget to add spikes. Create a mini garden or desert scene by building other types of cacti, with or without spikes, and any other features you might find there.

TRY THIS!

☐ Add some brightly coloured flowers.
☐ Build a LEGO pot for the cactus, in bright Mexican-style colours and patterns.

LEGO Language

Cheese slope
(noun) *say* cheez slohp

The fan name for the sloped LEGO **part** 'Roof Tile 1x1x2/3', so called because these pieces in yellow look like — and have been used in sets as — a wedge of cheese. Not to be confused with the Cooper's Hill cheese-rolling event in Gloucestershire, England.

Classic
(proper noun, adjective) *say* klasik

In **AFOL** terms, Classic refers to the original range of LEGO sets, such as the Space and Castle sets from the 1970s and 1980s. See also **Neo-Classic**. LEGO now uses Classic as a name for the range of basic brick sets.

CASTLE

Always grand and expansive buildings, castles are a firm favourite for LEGO builders. Some are home to noble families, large armies, wizards, vampires, mad scientists, dragons, goblins, elves, or Unicorn Kitten Princesses. They can be made to look like stone and wood; have fancy arches and spires, lookouts and towers, marble and statues, drawbridges and moats; they can be twisty and fairytale, high-tech and futuristic or even rundown and spooky.

Try making your own castle and give it some of the features above. You can copy a real castle, one from a story, or make up your own towering creation. Start by gathering all your LEGO together, then consider what size castle you can make from the pieces you have and what colours you think it will be.

TRY THIS!

- ☐ If you don't have tons of LEGO, build your castle in **microscale**.
- ☐ Castles are often built on top of hills or mountains. Build the landscape as well.
- ☐ Does your castle have a drawbridge?

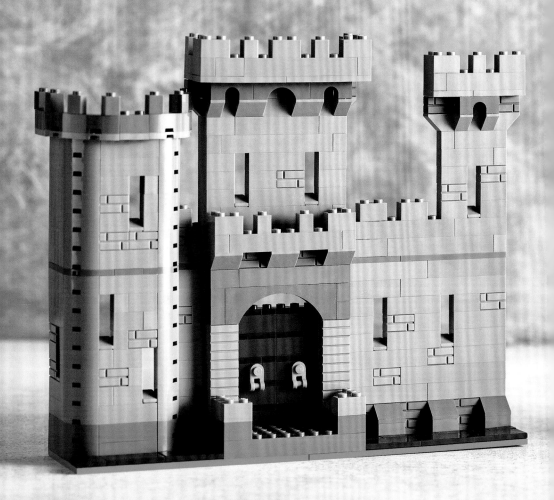

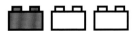

COASTERS

Make some LEGO **brick** coasters for putting your drinks on. You can make them smooth by using **tiles**, so your cup has a flat surface to sit on. Make patterns or pictures with the tiles to personalise them.

TRY THIS!

- [ ] Personalise your coasters by building your initials into them.
- [ ] Make coasters for special occasions such as birthdays, celebrations or Christmas.
- [ ] Go large-scale and make a matching placemat.
- [ ] Rather than building your coasters with flat plates topped with tiles, make a flat surface with bricks laid sideways.

LEGO Language

Clip
(noun) *say* klip

A term to describe the U-shaped part of some LEGO **elements** that can connect to the standard LEGO **bar**.

(verb)
Describes the action of connecting a U-shaped part (either on a LEGO element or **minifigure** hand) to a standard LEGO bar.

Clutch power
(noun) *say* kluch powuh

Describes the tendency of LEGO pieces to stay together when the **anti-studs** on the bottom grip onto the **studs** on the top. It is also the name of a character in an animated LEGO movie.

COMIC

Make a short comic using your favourite **minifigures** doing something cool or funny. Decide on a story, then pose minifigs in the scenes you build. Take photographs of the important moments to tell the story with the pictures. Use minifig heads with different expressions to convey how the characters are feeling. If you have photo-editing software you could add speech bubbles digitally or print your pictures and stick on your own speech bubbles.

TRY THIS!

☐ Write the story first and sketch out each scene.
☐ Build backgrounds (see **Perspective** on page 218).

LEGO Language

Connection
(noun) *say* kuhnekshuhn

A sturdy way to join LEGO **parts** by either clicking, snapping or studding in place.

Connector peg
(noun) *say* kuhnektuh peg

This is a small LEGO piece used to pin **Technic**™ holes together. There are three main types: 1- or 2-**stud** length with a stud on one end, standard 2-stud length and a longer 3-stud length. There are other variations, including ones with extra friction or no friction, or that are half-cross axle pins. *Also known as*: Technic pins.

CRAZY GOLF

Time for some crazy minigolf! Use LEGO **baseplates**, **plates** and **tiles** to create a minigolf course that you can actually play on. You can use LEGO balls if you have them, or even marbles, although they will be harder to move around your course because they are heavier. Use **slopes** and rounded pieces to create borders so that the balls won't fly off the edges, then create obstacles for your course. Look at real minigolf courses for inspiration. Try powering up your creations with **Technic** motors for added movement and challenge, but be sure to gear down your motors otherwise they'll be way too fast.

TRY THIS!

☐ Don't have enough tiles to cover the **studs**? Build walls and obstacles on your floor. Create a U-shaped wall as the hole.

☐ Your course can be 3D too: try adding height with ramps and tunnels.

LEGO Language

Corner brick
(noun) *say* kawnuh brik

A 2x2 **brick** that has one corner removed to make a distinctive L-shape. These are used for making **connections** between perpendicular walls and structures. *Also known as*: Ls.

PRO TECHNIQUE
COLOUR

LEGO **parts** now come in more than 50 different colours, and one of the most important ways you can improve your LEGO skills is by getting to know the colours and how you can use them. Colours that contrast, such as blue and white, can be used to emphasise shapes and create patterns.

Most natural surfaces are a mixture of colours, but with LEGO it's best to stick to two colours that are similar, but not too similar; for example, the light and dark versions of a colour work well together to simulate natural variation of shades.

SPEEDY STRIPES

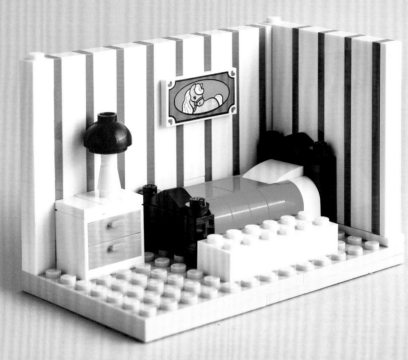

CONTRAST COLOURS

LIGHT AND DARK SIMULATE STONE

SHADES OF GREEN

D is for...

DEMOLITION

Try building something that looks impressive, but would look even better being destroyed! Building something strong enough to stay up and look good, but also to fall apart in a spectacular way, is actually quite hard. One trick is to make your building a big empty box, using large panels or stacks of **bricks** that are only held together with one LEGO® **stud** at the top, and then filling the space inside with loose LEGO pieces, like a piñata. Another way is to make something tall or high that is held up only by a single LEGO piece or section that you can pull out to make it fall over.

TRY THIS!

☐ Theme your build: make an explosion in a fireworks factory or blow the top off a popcorn machine.

BEFORE

DESSERT

What's your favourite sweet treat? Is it a big bowl of fruit salad? Or maybe a delicious ice-cream cone? Try building it from LEGO. Do your best to make the colours match the food; for example, if it's chocolate, use brown pieces. If your dessert needs a bowl or plate, you can use a real one, or for an extra challenge, you could build them out of LEGO too.

TRY THIS!

☐ For even more of a challenge, try building LEGO cutlery to go with your dessert.

☐ Making food from LEGO is a great opportunity for **N.P.U.** Tree leaves can become lettuce, for example.

LEGO Language

Design I.D.
(noun) *say* duhzuyn uy-dee

The number LEGO gives to each new type of **part** it produces. The design I.D. is moulded onto each piece, but it can be difficult to read and find. *See also* **element**.

Dinosaur
(noun) *say* duynuhsaw

LEGO has made dinosaurs in their sets for more than 20 years, with the first simple moulded dinosaurs in Adventurers sets in 2000. Since then, LEGO has created much more complex and posable dinosaurs with click **joints** and **Technic™** pin **connections**.

DICE TOWER

Are you tired of losing your dice when playing board games? Well, with a LEGO dice tower you'll never need to worry about losing them again! A dice tower is like a tall box with stepped **bricks** inside to make the dice tumble and roll as they fall through the tower. Add some clear windows so you can watch the dice fall through. You will need to make sure the gaps in the tower are big enough for the dice to roll smoothly to the bottom.

TRY THIS!

☐ Use **bricks** and **slopes** to make steps and ramps within the tower that make the dice roll and spin as they tumble through it.

☐ You can theme your dice tower to match your favourite game.

LEGO Language

Diorama
(noun) *say* duyuhrahmah

A term used to describe a scene built with 3D figures or **elements**, such as the Villain's lair on page 292. A diorama can be created using LEGO **bricks**, either with **minifigs** or larger **brick-built** elements on a base.

Dish
(noun) *say* dish

Called either a 'parabola' or 'satellite dish' by LEGO, these round LEGO pieces look like flattened bowls. Usually with a central **stud** or hole, they come in a variety of sizes, from two LEGO studs to 10 LEGO studs in diameter.

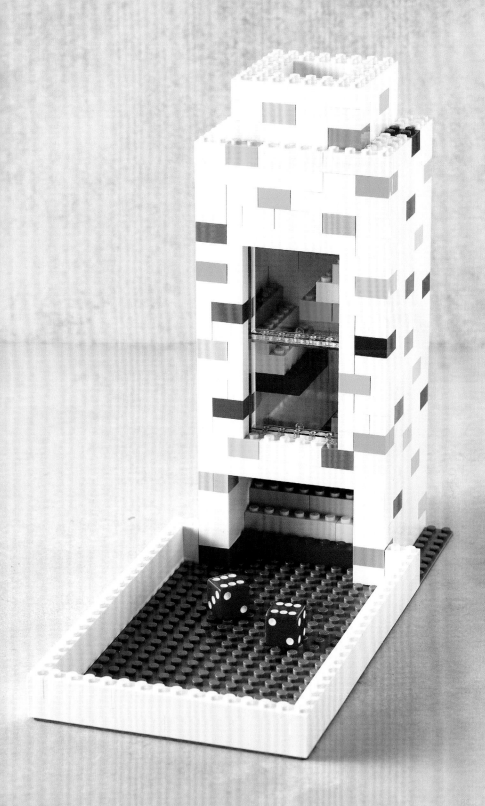

DINOSAUR

Everyone loves dinosaurs, whether they are scary carnivores like T-rex or graceful flying pterosaurs. What's your favourite kind?

LEGO has some ready-made **dinosaurs** in its sets, but you can also make your own from LEGO **bricks**. Start with the dinosaur's shape: does it have four legs or two? How big is its head? If you have LEGO ball or click **joint** pieces you could use them to give your dinosaur movable legs or a tail.

Be sure to capture whatever features make your dinosaur unique: does it have lots of teeth and tiny arms like a T-rex? Or does it have a frill and horns like a triceratops? LEGO makes lots of horn and spike pieces that you can use to give the dinosaur these features, or you could use **minifig accessories** – such as swords – as horns too. That's **N.P.U.**

Recently scientists have discovered that many dinosaurs had feathers and probably came in lots of colours, so don't be afraid to decorate your dinosaur models with cool patterns and different LEGO pieces.

TRY THIS!

☐ A dinosaur's head is usually the most distinctive part, which makes it a good place to start.
☐ Find a LEGO piece that represents a feature of the dinosaur, and use it to work out the scale to build it.
☐ If your dinosaur has two legs and a long tail, balance (see pages 38–39) is important.

DRAW

How creative can you get with LEGO? Try drawing a picture – of anything at all – and then recreating it with LEGO **parts**. For an even bigger challenge, try recreating an old drawing, or get someone else to draw something for you to build. Once you have mastered this, have a competition with family or friends to see who can recreate the best drawing.

TRY THIS!

☐ If you're trying to recreate an odd shape from the drawing, lay the LEGO pieces over the top loosely to see if you can match the outline.

☐ Do your best to match the colours of the original, but don't worry if you can't: LEGO only comes in a limited number of colours, after all!

☐ Expand the challenge and try to bring the drawing to life in 3D.

LEGO Language

DUPLO®
(noun) *say* dyooh·ploh

LEGO's name for their range of larger **bricks** and **parts** designed for babies and toddlers up to five years of age. They actually work with LEGO bricks, with the tubes on the underside of LEGO bricks fitting into the hollow **studs** of DUPLO. Each DUPLO stud is the same size as a 2x2 LEGO brick.

PRO TECHNIQUE
DIGITAL

There are a number of computer software programs available that let you design and build LEGO models digitally, the best known of which are LEGO's own LEGO Digital Designer (LDD), and Bricklink's Studio. Unfortunately, LDD is no longer being supported by LEGO, but you can still download and use it for free. Studio is also free and is kept up to date, with new **parts** and colours added frequently.

Building digitally can be a great way to go if you don't have lots of your own LEGO **bricks**, or just want to try out some new LEGO **connections** and parts. These programs also allow you to use parts in colours that don't exist in real life LEGO, which can be really fun!

ACTUAL BUILD

BRICKLINK STUDIO DIGITAL BUILD

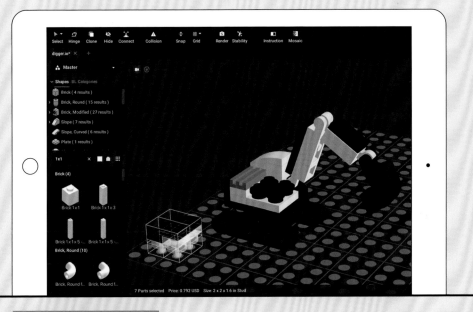

TRY OUT NEW PARTS AND CONNECTIONS ON SCREEN

E is for...

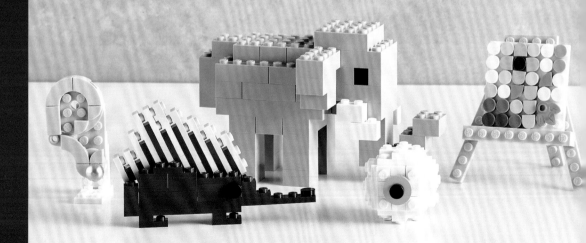

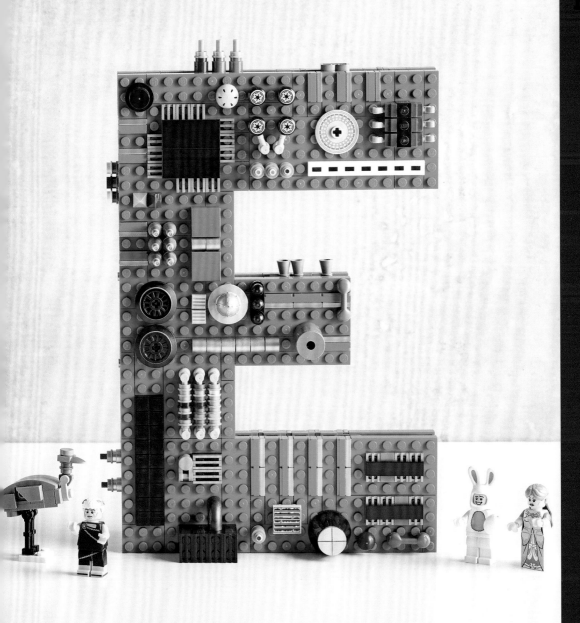

ENERGY

There are lots of ways to supply power to towns: electricity, wind power, nuclear fission, hydro-electricity or even solar power. But LEGO® towns can be powered by anything you like! Make a kooky power station that runs on something weird: how about hamsters in wheels, or cow poo, or garbage, or a giant electric eel?

TRY THIS!

- ☐ If an animal powers your energy machine, make sure it has food.
- ☐ Add movement with **Powered UP**™, **Power Functions** or **Technic**™.
- ☐ Create a vehicle with an engine that runs on your kooky power source.

VOLUTION

LEGO evolution is the survival of the brickest or, at least, the best built. Make several models of the same thing that improve with each version. Start simple and easy, then improve on the previous build again and again until you have a well-built and complex model. For example, start with a basic robot, then improve it by adding extra joints and features and more decoration. The next model could even have wings and a radio transmitter. Display them all together to show how your ideas evolved.

TRY THIS!

- ☐ It can help to sketch out the idea on paper or a computer first.
- ☐ Start with an important detail of the build, or the frame it will be built on.
- ☐ If you don't have enough LEGO to display all the evolutions together, take photos to show how it progressed instead.

Element
(noun) *say* eluhmuhnt

This is the name LEGO gives to each different type of **part** it produces. As well as the different shapes, each coloured version of a part has its own unique element I.D. number; although they have the same **design I.D.** a red 2x4 **brick** has a different element I.D. from a blue 2x4 brick.

EXPERT

Creativity is like a muscle that must be flexed regularly to keep it healthy and happy. A good way to increase your expertise with LEGO is to try something new. If you're used to building one kind of object at a comfortable level of difficulty, try building something more complex. Add more detail, change the scale, make it work more realistically, and push your knowledge and techniques to become more expert.

TRY THIS!

- [ ] Use LEGO **Technic** to create stronger frames for larger builds and to add motors for movement.
- [ ] Look online for inspiration: you'll find tons of amazing LEGO blogs and builders' websites.
- [ ] Keep trying if a build doesn't work the first time.

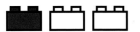

XPLORE

The spirit of adventure lies in us all, so create an environment for your **minifigures** to explore. It could be ancient jungle ruins, a weird alien world or a fun adventure park: LEGO can take you to some strange and wonderful places! Hide some treasure behind a waterfall or in a mountainside cave, make puzzles and traps to navigate, and fill the area with plenty of secrets to discover. Pretend you are on a mission to find artefacts before your arch-nemesis gets there first.

TRY THIS!

☐ Start by making an explorer minifig: make them the coolest you can and ensure they have all the right equipment.
☐ Build the ground up with hidden details underneath.
☐ Add **hinges** to your build so that walls, gates and trapdoors can open to reveal treasures or traps.

LEGO Language

Erling brick
(noun) *say* er-ling brik

A 1x1 **brick** that has an extra **stud** on one side of the brick and an **anti-stud** on the opposite side. It was designed by a LEGO employee named Erling Dideriksen. It is also called a **headlight brick** as its primary use was to add headlights to the front of vehicle builds.

EYEBALL

What could be spookier than a big gross eyeball? Make a sphere with a handful of **SNOT** bricks (see pages 258–259) and plenty of **plates**, then add details to make it spookier.

TRY THIS!

☐ Make it scary: try a vertical pupil and drips of transparent goo.
☐ Make it funny: use crazy colours and give it a googly pupil.

PRO TECHNIQUE ENGINE

LEGO has lots of ways to add complexity and functionality to your models, and one that's fun and interesting to try is adding a LEGO motor. Simulating an engine or natural movement can be done easily if you add in the right components to make the action work. You can drive wheels, make remote-control steering, attach a crank shaft, attach **gears** and much more. If you can think of a movement you want to achieve, it's quite possible to do it with motors.

AUTO-WAVE MACHINE

F is for...

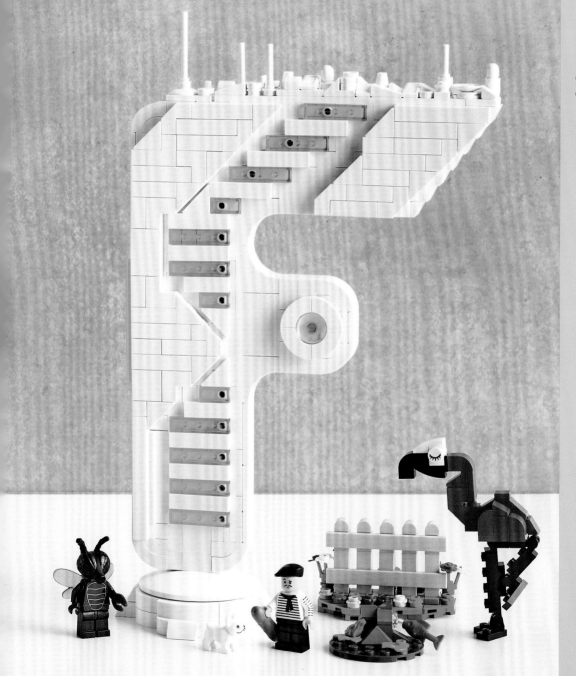

FACTORY

Create a factory that puts something together on an assembly line. Try to tell the story of how the factory's product is made and bring it to life with **minifigs**. If you have some LEGO® **Technic**™, you can even make parts of the assembly line move.

TRY THIS!

- [ ] There are lots of factory assembly line videos you can look at online for inspiration.
- [ ] Make a delivery vehicle to take the product to stores.
- [ ] Rebuild your factory as if something went wrong. What if the bottle-capping machine got jammed?

F

FAIRY

What do you think a fairy looks like? Does it have butterfly wings? Or antlers like a deer? Are fairies green like the forest they live in, or pink like the flowers of the meadows? See what LEGO colours you have and try to make the most colourful fairy you can, or you could create a place for your fairy to live.

TRY THIS!

☐ Fairies aren't always good. Build a bad fairy or their house.
☐ Fairies are usually associated with nature, so you could also build them an animal friend as their pet.
☐ If you're stuck for ideas, make a character from a fairytale.

LEGO Language

Fabuland
(noun) *say* fabyoohland

The name of a LEGO theme for younger builders that ran from 1979 to 1989. The range included non-**minifig** characters with different animal heads such as Leonard Lion and Elmer Elephant. It also featured several large specially moulded pieces, mostly in primary colours.

Flex tube
(noun) *say* fleks-tyoohb

A LEGO **part** which is the same diameter as a standard **bar**, but is hollow and flexible and comes in some sets in a variety of lengths. One of the few LEGO parts that many **AFOLs** are happy to cut to size, as early sets that included it did in fact give directions to cut it to the required length.

F

87

FARM

Build a small farm scene where the farmers are growing something or raising animals, but make it as absurd or interesting as you can. Imagine what a field of ice-cream plants or a flying-pig farm would look like … then build it! Farms are a great setting for LEGO models: they're always a hive of activity with lots of cool special vehicles, different types of buildings, opportunities for stories with **minifigs** and chances to build different types of plants or animals.

TRY THIS!

- [ ] If your farm is growing an unusual crop, think about what kind of special vehicles might be needed for harvesting, or what buildings might be needed for storage.
- [ ] If your farm is raising a special type of animal (such as a golden egg-laying goose), make sure the farm has food for them and that there are ways to stop them running (or flying) away.

LEGO Language

F.L.U.
(noun) *say* ef-el-yooh

F.L.U. stands for Fundamental LEGO Unit, and equates to the width and length of a 1x1 LEGO **plate** or **brick**. It is useful for calculating LEGO maths (see page 166).

Flush
(noun) *say* flush

When two LEGO **parts**' surfaces align to form a straight line or create a seamless surface, they are flush.

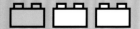

FRANKENLEGO

One of the greatest things about LEGO is that it's endlessly adaptable and can bring to life things that otherwise only exist in our imaginations. So why not take two or more of your favourite things and build something from LEGO **bricks** that combines them? It could be a shark and a motorcycle, or a bunny with hair and a unicorn horn. Or you could mash-up your favourite LEGO themes into one crazy vehicle or building: imagine if your house was a swimming pool and you swam from room to room instead of walking. Imagine it, then get building!

TRY THIS!

☐ Sketch your ideas out on paper before you start to build. This can help you visualise how best to combine things.

☐ Get someone else to decide the things you must combine.

Would you ride
my shark bike?

FUTURE

Have a look at an everyday activity or object and imagine how it might be done in the future; for example, you could make a dog-pooper-scooper robot or a solar-powered plane.

TRY THIS!

☐ A lot of inventions help people do jobs they don't enjoy: think of a task you don't like and invent a machine to do it instead.

☐ Make your build use renewable energy, such as wind or solar.

PRO TECHNIQUE
FILLERS

Often in a build there can be gaps between odd angles of LEGO pieces, when we simply don't have a piece that's the right size to create the solid lines or surfaces we're trying to make. This is when knowing about 'filler' **parts** and how to attach them can help.

Lots of small LEGO pieces can be fillers: the 1x1x2/3 **slope** (or **cheese slope**) is a great one, as are 1x1 or 1x2 panels, which can slide over the top of irregular edges or cover up a random **stud** that's facing the wrong direction. **Brackets** and **SNOT bricks** can be used to attach filler pieces sideways, too.

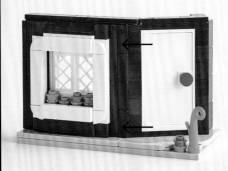

CHEESE SLOPES

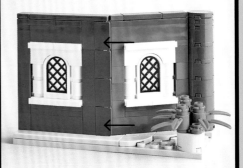

1X2 PANELS

G is for...

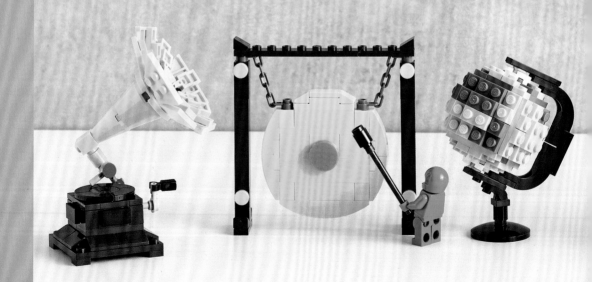

G

GAME

Have you ever wanted to create your own board game? You can make props and pieces out of LEGO® and customise them as much as you like. Make a board on a **baseplate**, markers and dice, scenery to set the stage, spinners, cards – let your imagination run wild.

TRY THIS!

☐ If you're not sure where to start, copy a favourite board game.
☐ There are lots of LEGO game ideas in *Brickman's Family Challenge Book*, including how to make dice and spinners!

LEGO Language

Galidor
(proper noun) *say* galuhdaw

One of the first LEGO set ranges made to accompany a TV series, Galidor is notorious among **AFOL**s because of how 'un-LEGO' it was. The sets were mostly large action figures, joined together with click **hinges**. The hero of the sets and TV series, Nick Bluetooth, was named after a Danish king, Harald 'Bluetooth'.

Garbage build
(noun) *say* gahbij bild

When you build your own LEGO creations you inevitably end up with **parts** lying around that you didn't use. A garbage build is something you make from these parts. It is not normally intended as a finished creation. Can also be a small build made out of the spare parts left over from building an official LEGO set. Should not be confused with a **tablescrap**, though a garbage build can develop into a tablescrap.

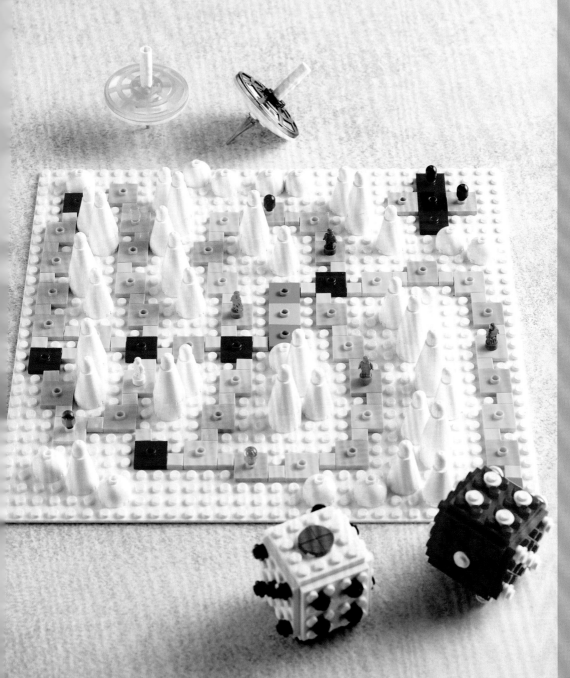

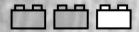

GARDEN

A garden is a great place to relax and enjoy nature; the colours and fresh air are peaceful and improve your mood. You can make your own miniature garden to decorate a windowsill or table in your house. LEGO comes in lots of wonderful colours that you can mix and match for interesting plants and flowers. Give them petals and leaves using **clips** and **hinges** so you can pose them at natural angles. Make a little container to match the décor of the room you will display the garden in, and arrange the plants to show off each one. Match the colours and function of the room in the design, and use regular plant pieces as filler around the base of your plant builds to make denser greenery.

TRY THIS!

- [ ] If you don't have the **parts** to make big plants, make a **microscale** garden.
- [ ] Place some landscaping in your garden with rocks, pathways and ponds.
- [ ] Add animals and insects to the garden.

Garden Gnome

No garden would be complete without a trusty gnome standing guard. Make a gnome for your yard and personalise it to suit your family. You could even give the gnome something to do, such as digging, fishing, mining, sunbathing, mowing or whatever you like. Once you've filled your garden with gnomes, make a few smaller ones to place in the pot plants around your home, or make a miniature gnome for your LEGO garden (see page 98).

TRY THIS!

- ☐ Give your gnome personality with printed LEGO eye **tiles**.
- ☐ You don't have to build your gnome with a hat and beard. What do you think a female gnome might look like? Or a baby gnome? Make your gnome look the way you want it to.
- ☐ Expand your gnome's world by adding other LEGO props, scenery or creatures for them to interact with.

LEGO Language

Gear
(noun) *say gear*

LEGO **Technic**™ includes round pieces with interlocking teeth that are called gears. These allow the user to build in movement and interactive elements, but they can be used as decorative elements as well.

GARLAND

Create a decorative garland for a special occasion by making festive shapes and stringing them together. The shapes can be any size you like; just be sure to include a way to hang them. Choose a theme: stars and moons, hearts, pumpkins and bats, balloons, candy canes, flowers, UFOs or just about anything.

TRY THIS!

☐ Use LEGO string **parts** with built-in **bars** for clipping parts on.
☐ Some LEGO parts have holes that you can thread string or ribbon through. Take a close look at the parts you have.
☐ You can make a garland for your room, but don't make the decorations too heavy.

LEGO Language

Greeble
(noun) *say* greebuhl

Small pieces added to the flat surface of a LEGO build to break it up. This makes the model more visually interesting and convincing (see pages 106–107).

(verb)
To add greeble to the surface of an object. *Also known as*: nurnie.

Grill tile
(noun) *say* gril tuyl

A **tile** that has two slots cut into its surface so that it resembles a grill. Used to add features to buildings and vehicles. *Also known as*: barbecue.

GHOST

A fun way to spook your friends and family is to create a 'Pepper's ghost' illusion – a stage magic trick that uses mirrors to make an offstage actor appear as if they are a ghost on stage. Make a closed corridor with a person at one end; midway along the corridor add a windowpane placed diagonally so that it reflects a ghostly figure that you have placed down a side corridor. The ghostly figure reflects in the window and appears to be hovering beside the person at the end of the corridor.

TRY THIS!

- [ ] Show the trick to your family and friends and see if they can work it out!
- [ ] Use a light brick (see page 167) to light up the hidden figure.
- [ ] Put the ghost trick in a haunted house.

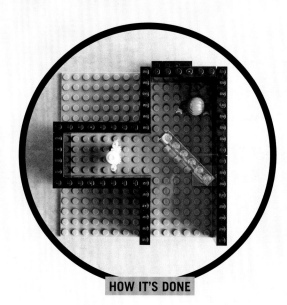

HOW IT'S DONE

Is someone there? Knock twice for yes.

PRO TECHNIQUE
GREEBLING

Greebling is a technique where small **parts** (**greebles** or nurnies) are added to the surface of larger models to make them appear more complex and detailed. When building larger models, it can be difficult to keep them visually interesting, especially when you have a large area of studded surfaces that, even though they create a pattern, aren't in themselves very exciting. Lots of smaller objects arranged on the surface can make it seem like there's more going on in the structure, without having to build complex interiors.

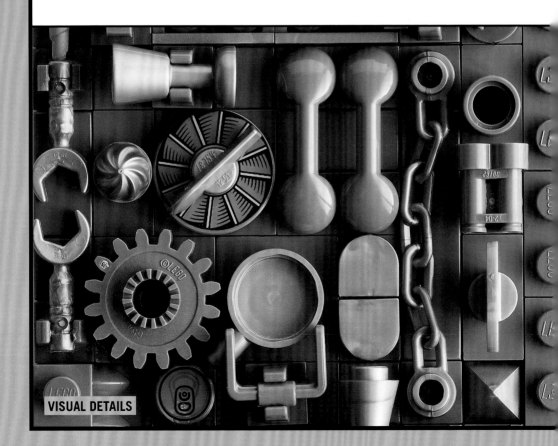

VISUAL DETAILS

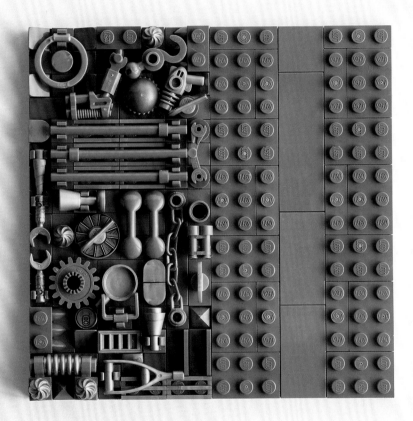

GREEBLES OR NURNIES

H is for...

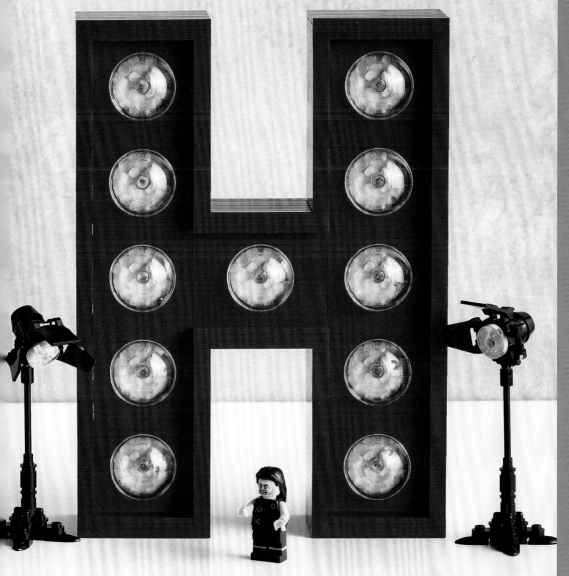

H

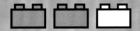

HALLOWEEN

Halloween provides a treasure trove of inspiration for terrifying builds. A number of LEGO® **minifigs** come with alternative 'scared' faces, so why not try and build something spooky for them to be scared of? It could be a creepy house with pop-up ghosts, or a monster to chase them. You could build your own LEGO Halloween decorations too, from a giant LEGO spider to frighten your friends, to a LEGO pumpkin to put in your window.

TRY THIS!

☐ Did you know that LEGO makes glow-in-the-dark pieces? If you have any, use them to add an extra level of spookiness.

☐ Add some simple mechanisms to make your ghosts 'pop out' and scare your minifigs!

APPARITION

POP-UP COFFIN LID

HELPER

Wouldn't it be great to have your own personal helper, someone to do all your chores for you? Build a remote-control lawnmower, a machine to feed your pet, a magical dragon who washes the dishes, a robot that finds missing socks, a fairy with a room-tidying wand or a computer that does your homework for you.

TRY THIS!

☐ Think about the chore you need your LEGO helper to do, and make sure they have the right tools to do it. They could be robot scooping hands or a sock-finding radar.

☐ Give your helper a name, and maybe even build it a home where it can recharge between chores!

LEGO Language

Half-stud
(adjective) *say* hahf-stud

A measurement of distance in LEGO constructions. Correlates with half an **F.L.U.** and is typically created with a **jumper plate**. *See also* LEGO maths (page 166).

Headlight brick
(noun) *say* hedluyt brik

A 1x1-**stud brick** with a stud on one vertical side. *Also known as*: washing machine brick or **Erling brick**.

HIDEOUT

Create a secret hideout for a **minifig** to run away to. Don't forget to include a concealed entrance and a back door for quick escapes, as well as whatever things your minifig likes best.

TRY THIS!

- ☐ Use LEGO **hinges** to make secret doors that can easily open and close.
- ☐ Make sure the entrances and exits are well hidden. Make them the same colour as the walls, or cover them with LEGO plants.
- ☐ Bring your hideout to life with minifigs hiding and seeking.

H

LEGO Language

Hinge
(noun) *say* hinj

These LEGO **parts** can be connected and then moved on a single axis or rotated. Hinges can be **bricks** and **plates** with a variety of mechanisms. They are useful for making doors as well as complex geometric shapes. *See also* **angles** (page 24).

Homemaker
(proper noun) *say* hohm-maykuh

Homemaker was the name of a LEGO set range available from 1971 through to 1982. It featured large basic **brick-built** figures, which had large moulded heads, hairpieces and movable arms that connected with ball **joints**.

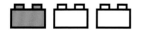

Holiday

Where would you love to go for a holiday? A golden beach? A snowy mountain? Or maybe even outer space? Dream up the best holiday destination you can imagine, then build it from LEGO. Don't forget to include yourself and your family and friends enjoying your LEGO holiday. Make it fun and let your imagination go wild as you create a holiday to remember! It's not every day you get to go on a jungle jaunt or a safari, but with LEGO there's no reason not to.

TRY THIS!

- ☐ Ask your friends and family what they'd like to do on a holiday and try to add them as **minifigs** to bring the scene to life.
- ☐ How will you get to your dream holiday destination? Build a vehicle (boat, plane, train or spaceship) that will get you there!
- ☐ Make it **minifigure scale**, or make it as big as you like.

LEGO Language

Hose
(noun) *say* hohz

LEGO **parts** that replicate flexible pipes. Not to be confused with **flex tube**, hoses normally come with standard **connections** at the ends that are designed to attach to a LEGO **stud**, or clip into a standard LEGO **clip**.

Home

Try to build a replica of your home in LEGO. Start by mapping (see pages 180–181) the basic outline of your home on paper, working out how many rooms you have and how many windows and doors there are. Then transfer the layout to a LEGO **baseplate** and start building. Don't forget the toilet!

TRY THIS!

☐ You don't have to build your home in **minifig scale**. You can build it at whatever scale you like, just as long as you can recognise it as your home.

PRO TECHNIQUE
HOLLOW

H

Leaving the inside of a model hollow is an important technique to learn as you start building bigger models. Filling the model with **bricks** takes longer and wastes LEGO inside, when it could be going into making it bigger and better on the outside.

Build the outer walls of the model as strongly as you can (see tips on page 295), and then try to connect each outer wall to its opposite side with long bridges of LEGO bricks or **plates**. This is called 'bracing'. You only need to do this every few layers of bricks, but it will make your LEGO builds stronger, and you'll be able to make them even bigger, as you'll have more bricks to go on the outside.

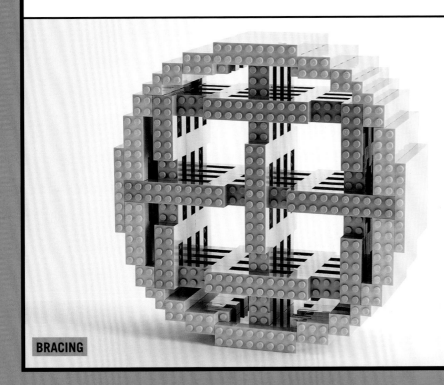

BRACING

I is for...

ICE CREAM

Build your own ice-cream dream. Make a model of a delicious looking dessert (and don't forget the toppings)! Use **SNOT** bricks (see page 248) and colourful 1x1 round **plates** or **tiles** to create sprinkles. Make the top brown if you like chocolate fudge sauce.

TRY THIS!

- ☐ Fairy floss cloud flavour? Unicorn sprinkles? Rainbow chocolate? Lightning berry topping? Yes please!
- ☐ If you'd rather eat a sundae than a cone, make a bowl and spoon to match your flavour choice.

I

Heaven
in a cone!

ILLUSION

You can recreate heaps of optical illusions using LEGO® **bricks**. By building shapes and viewing them from a different angle, they can appear to defy physics. The main trick to creating these is to make sure the build is only viewed from the angle that makes the illusion work. Build a wall with a hole in it in front of the model that people can look through to see the illusion. Or photograph the model from the correct angle and see how many of your friends you can fool.

TRY THIS!

- ☐ Look at drawings and paintings by M.C. Escher for inspiration.
- ☐ Make sure that the surfaces you want to appear as though they are joined are the same colour and texture.

LEGO Language

Illegal
(adjective) *say* ileeguhl

This refers to any **connection** frowned upon by LEGO, as it may stress, strain or break the LEGO pieces. But what you do with your LEGO **bricks** is your own business. *See also* illegal Pro Technique (page 129).

Inventory
(noun) *say* inventuhree

A visual list of LEGO **parts** needed to complete a model. An inventory is usually found either in the instruction booklet that comes with a set or on the outside of the box.

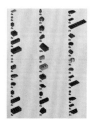

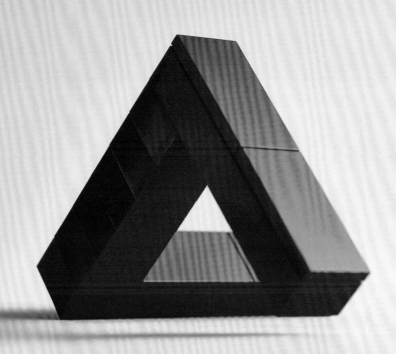

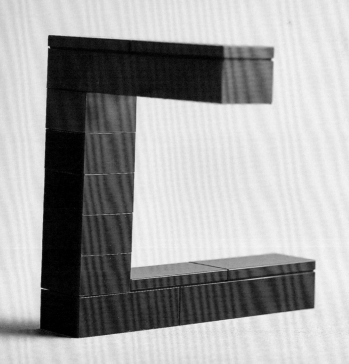

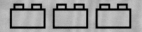

INTERIOR

Have you ever thought what it would be like if a **minifigure** lived inside an everyday object from our world? They are a lot smaller than us, so they could fit easily inside lots of different things: an apple, a soft-drink can, a teddy bear, a teapot, a lamp, a shoe, a cuckoo clock, an alarm clock, etc. Build the object as close as you can to life-size, but make the interior of it a little house for a minifigure. You could leave the back side of the object open like a doll's house so that you can play with the minifig. It can be as whimsical and weird as you like and include as many fun things as you wish. Maybe add a hidden door as an entry, and strategically placed windows as features of the object.

TRY THIS!

- ☐ Make the object transform into a vehicle. Put fold-out **wheels** underneath, or add a pop-up jet engine.
- ☐ Think about what kind of tiny person would live in your object. Theme the inside to match.

INVENTION

LEGO isn't just for play and decoration; you can make useful things with it as well. Create a model that does a simple task, such as folding your socks or pressing your snooze button. Any problem can be solved with ingenuity.

TRY THIS!

- [ ] Investigate using **Technic**™, **gears** and **Powered UP**™ or **Power Functions** motors to make your invention move.
- [ ] Your invention doesn't have to be complicated: it could be as simple as a tripwire that pulls a bucket of LEGO onto the floor as an alarm.

PRO TECHNIQUE
ILLEGAL

There are certain **connections** that LEGO considers '**illegal**' because they might stress your **bricks** and bend them, but some of these can be quite useful when creating models. Most of the time LEGO is perfect for making the forms that you need, but now and then there will be a form that isn't possible with the existing **parts** you have on hand, and this may be where an illegal technique can be used to great effect. One of the most common ones is placing a **plate** sideways between **studs**, as shown lower left, centre.

I

ILLEGAL CONNECTIONS

MAKE IT FIT

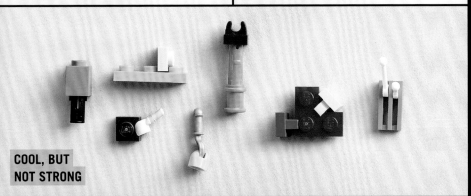

COOL, BUT NOT STRONG

J is for...

JACK-IN-THE-BOX

Using elastic bands or LEGO® **Technic**™ springs, you can make a jack-in-the-box to surprise your friends and family. Once you've created a box and pop-up mechanism, you can decorate it with any surprise you want: it could be a funny face, a cute animal or a scary monster.

TRY THIS!

☐ Make sure that the catch is strong enough to hold the lid closed when the elastics or springs are set.

☐ If you don't have the **parts** to make the lid pop up, just make a surprise in a box.

TECHNIC LIFTARMS IN CLOSED POSITION

THE ARMS PIVOT UPWARDS WHEN THE HANDLE IS TURNED

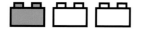

Jet

Build a jet plane from LEGO. It could be a passenger plane or a fighter jet, based on a real plane or just one you dream up — as long as it has jets at the back, go for it!

TRY THIS!

- [ ] Did you know that LEGO **wheel** hubs make great jet engines?
- [ ] Most jet engines need air intakes, so try to make sure that your jet-powered model has some.
- [ ] Your model doesn't have to be a flying vehicle. It could be a jet-powered car or boat, or even a jet pack you can wear.

LEGO Language

Janky
(adjective, adverb)
say jangkee

A wobbly or unstable LEGO **connection**. Usage: 'That's a janky tree. The branch is about to fall off.'

Joint
(noun) *say* joynt

Any movable **connection** between two or more LEGO **elements**. It can be as simple as a **plate** swivelling on a **stud**, or it could be one of several types of joints using different types of **hinges**. Types of joint can include ball joints, click joints, **Technic** pin and beam joints or **geared** Technic joints.

JIGSAW

LEGO now has a huge array of **parts** that use **clip**-and-**bar connections**. Use these to create a model in sections that can be pulled apart and clipped back together. The clips and bars could be hidden behind the surface of the model, or incorporated into the model's finish. The final model could be anything you like, 3D or flat. Pull it apart and challenge your family and friends to put it back together.

TRY THIS!

- [ ] Build the pieces in irregular shapes, such as L shapes or, for a real challenge, triangles!
- [ ] Make your jigsaw tougher with a confusing pattern on top.
- [ ] Make sure the clips and bars are securely built into each piece by sandwiching them between two **plates**, as shown below.

UNDERNEATH

FINISHED

JUMBLE

Using LEGO, create three **SNOT** (see page 258) cubes with different images on each side. One cube should have faces, another bodies and a third legs. Each of the six sides should have a different variation, from regular human features to imaginary creatures. Then stack and rearrange them to form all sorts of weird people!

TRY THIS!

- ☐ Make each cube and each side as different as you can.
- ☐ Create different accessories you can add to your zany figures, such as hats or boots or objects you can clip on.

JUNGLE

The jungle is a fantastic place to set a story: it's full of colour, life and adventure. Try to imagine a jungle scene: it could be an explorer finding a lost temple, a family enjoying a secluded waterfall or maybe a forest filled with native creatures. Be sure to make use of the many LEGO plant **elements** to make the model really look lush.

TRY THIS!

☐ If you don't have special plant pieces, use any green **parts**.
☐ Make a space jungle, an underwater jungle or a fantasy jungle.

LEGO Language

Jumbo Bricks
(proper noun) *say* jumboh briks

Jumbo Bricks were three times the size of regular LEGO **bricks** and designed for children aged three to five years. They came out in brick packs between 1966 and 1972. They paved the way for **DUPLO®**, which LEGO released later, in 1979.

Jumper plate
(noun) *say* jumpuh playt

A type of LEGO **plate** that has a **stud**, or studs, offset by half a stud from the normal alignment. As shown below, it might be a 1x2 plate with a single stud in the centre or a 1x3 plate with two studs offset in the centre, or similar configurations.

PRO TECHNIQUE
JIGSAW MOSAIC

The arrival of the **cheese slope** piece has meant LEGO builders have been able to incorporate much finer details into their builds. One of the most creative, but tricky, techniques the cheese slope allows is **SNOT** jigsaw mosaics like the ones shown here.

You start by creating a one-**brick** deep 'container' in the ground of your model, by raising the surrounding area by one brick plus one **plate**'s worth of height. Make sure you **tile** the bottom of the container to make it smooth and flat. You can then start laying the cheese slopes into patterns.

Strictly speaking, the cheese slopes are not attached to anything, but if you arrange them just right they will fill the container and stay in place due to friction. This same technique can be used with other LEGO pieces, such as flat tiles laid on their sides or even **bars** stood vertically, if your container is deep enough.

For added safety on smaller mosaics like this, you can SNOT-build a large clear panel like the 1x5x6 ones over the top, which will help keep the **parts** in place and still let you see the mosaic.

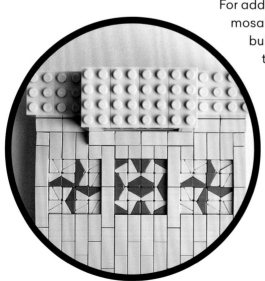

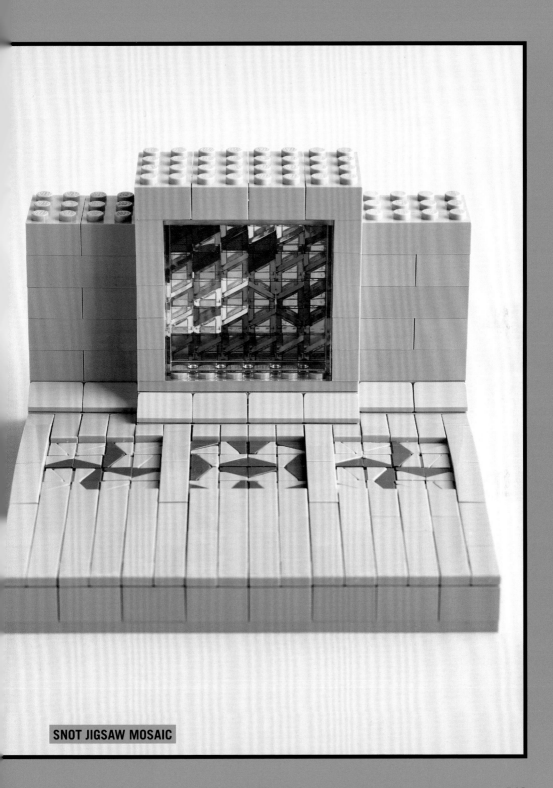

SNOT JIGSAW MOSAIC

J

K is for...

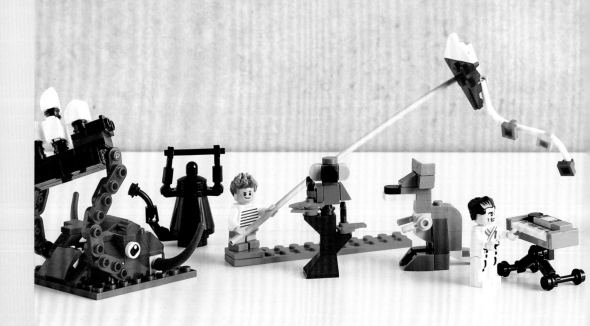

K

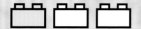

KALEIDOSCOPE

Create fun fractal patterns out of all kinds of LEGO® **parts**! Make a long rectangular tube, and use miniature mirror pieces or black panels as the reflective surface. You can insert one surface on an angle to make the reflections more complex. Then add a transparent floor to the bottom of the tube and a hole to look through the top. Gather together lots of small interesting bits of LEGO: transparent **studs**, dots, **tiles**, small detail pieces in various colours, small animals or decorative printed pieces. Put a few little pieces in the tube, shake it a little to shift them around and make awesome colourful patterns when you look through the peephole.

TRY THIS!

☐ Use as many big LEGO panel pieces for the tube as you can. If you don't have many, try to use large tiles or just the smooth sides of **bricks**.

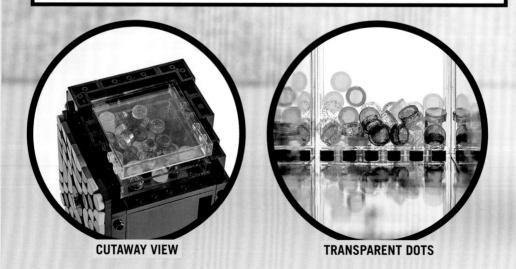

CUTAWAY VIEW   TRANSPARENT DOTS

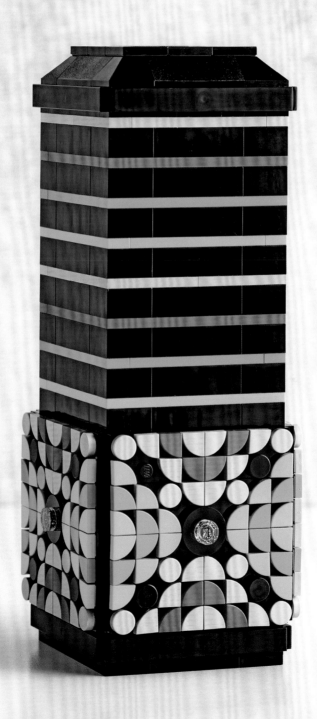

K

147

KEY

A fun challenge is creating a container that must be opened with a key or a secret hidden locking mechanism. It might be a treasure chest or a safe for your valuables, and only you will know how to open it up. Or you could try building a box that can only be opened with a key, to hide a gift for someone. Research how locks and puzzles work to get some ideas.

TRY THIS!

- ☐ The lock doesn't necessarily need to have a key – you can also lock a box with secret sliding pieces which will stop the lid from opening.
- ☐ Hide the locking piece behind its own secret door, or disguise it as part of the outside of the box.

LEGO Language

KFOL
(noun) *say* kay-fol

An acronym for Kid Fan Of LEGO. *See also* **AFOL** and **YFOL**.

Knob stone
(noun) *say* nob-stohn

The official LEGO name of the 1x1 **brick** that has hollow **studs** on all four side faces as well as the top. Its most common nickname is the **Travis brick**, after a LEGO fan who favoured this brick. *Also known as:* robot head, Dalek.

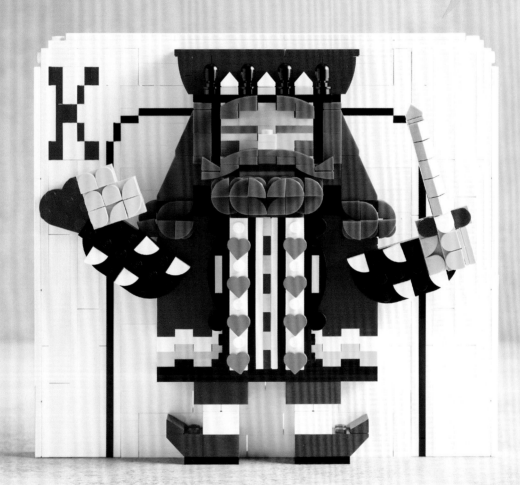

The king has
left the building.

KING

Long live the king! Build a king, whether it's the King of Fairyland, a king chess piece, the evil king of the goblin wizards, King Kong, the king of rock'n'roll or a king-size piece of cheese. It could be a king from a story you know, or your own creation.

TRY THIS!

- [ ] Every king needs a crown: it doesn't have to be gold, but it should look distinctive and special.
- [ ] If you're building a king-size build, plan ahead and make sure you have the quantity (see pages 228–229) of **parts** you need.
- [ ] Make sure your king looks the part with colourful robes and a distinctive weapon or feature to make him stand out.

K

LEGO Language

Knolling
(verb) *say* noling

Separating and organising the LEGO pieces for a particular build or set, by colour and piece to make it easier to find the parts needed as you advance through the building steps. Knolling can be loosely grouping parts into piles, or arranging them formally into a neat grid formation.

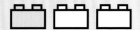

KNOCKER

There's nothing fancier than a personalised door knocker to let you know when visitors arrive. With a simple **hinge** mechanism, give your front door the flair you've been looking for with a LEGO doorknocker. It could be a lion's head, a gargoyle, a plant or anything you like. Use a simple **connection** to make the movable part that people use to knock, and attach the backing plate to your door with a removable adhesive pad.

TRY THIS!

- [ ] Remember that the parts of the knocker that will hit each other need to be strong enough to make a noise and not fall apart. Reinforce your knocker with **plates** or **Technic**™.
- [ ] You could personalise your knocker by writing your name on it with **SNOT** or plate lettering.

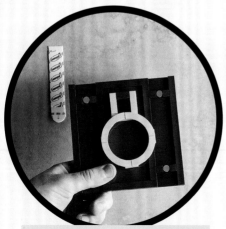

STICK ON WITH REMOVABLE PADS

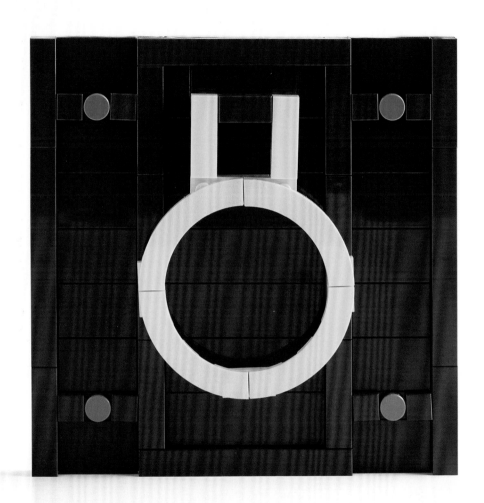

PRO TECHNIQUE
KABOOM!

An exciting feature to add to a build is an 'exploding' section, which will dismantle itself on command. Usually this is only held together with 1- or 2-**stud connections**, but the section itself is made up of larger, solidly built chunks. When the section is pushed or poked, it comes away from the studs and flies apart, giving the impression the build has broken, but then it can easily go back together again for another go! You could try making an exploding wall, or a collapsing tower.

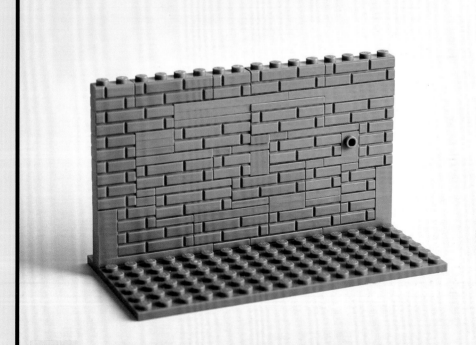

BEFORE

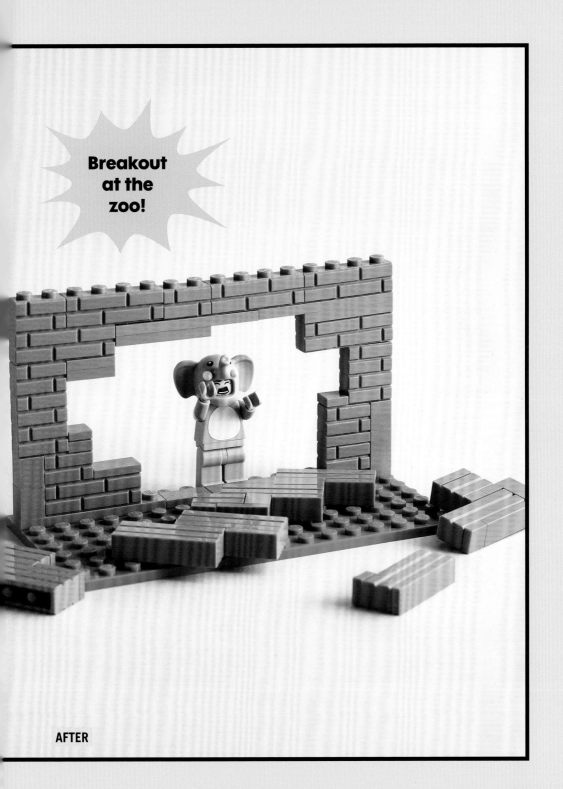

Breakout at the zoo!

K

AFTER

L is for...

LAUNCHER

Build a launcher out of LEGO® to fire a vehicle across the room! Use springs, long ramps, or even **Technic**™ motors and mechanisms to create a machine that will push or fire out a small LEGO vehicle piloted by a LEGO **minifigure**. Challenge your friends and see whose machine can launch their vehicle the furthest.

TRY THIS!

- Make your vehicle light and streamlined, with as little touching the ground as possible.
- If you're challenging your friends, don't forget to build a winners' podium and a trophy.

Away we gooooooo!

LEGS

Build a LEGO model with legs to keep it at least 15 cm (6 inches) off the ground. The more legs your model has, the easier it will be to stabilise. If you are adding joints to the legs, make sure that they are stiff enough to hold the weight of the model, so that they won't collapse (unless you want them to).

TRY THIS!

☐ For an extra challenge, try making the legs posable, or increasing the height to 30 cm (12 inches).

☐ Once you've mastered four or more legs, try building a model with just two legs!

LEGO Language

Leg godt
(adverbial phrase)
say luyh got

Meaning 'play well' in Danish, LEg GOdt is where the LEGO Group gets its name.

Legos
(not a real word)
say lay-gohz

This term is wrong, wrong, wrong! LEGO® is the brand name, not the name of an individual piece: you build with LEGO (it's both singular and plural, like 'fish' and 'sheep'), not legos, and if you want to talk about multiple pieces you can say LEGO **bricks**, LEGO **parts** or LEGO **accessories**. Always spell LEGO with all capital letters.

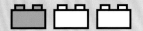

LIMOUSINE

Create a stretched version of something; a limousine is an extra-long car, but you could make a long plane, or even a long animal!

TRY THIS!

- ☐ Stretch your vehicle or creature in a different direction: imagine an extra-wide plane, or an extra-tall turtle.
- ☐ If you stretch your model out really long, remember that you might need to add some extra support halfway along, such as more **wheels** or extra legs.

Lifestyles of the rich and famous.

LUCKY DIP

Get a big tub and an assortment of LEGO **parts**. Or, if you have all of your LEGO in a tub already, you can just use that. Without looking, reach in and grab some random parts. Lay out the parts and see if they suggest anything to you: if you've got a steering wheel, maybe you could build some kind of car? Or if you have a horse you could build a Wild West wagon. You are allowed to choose more pieces to complete your build, if you need to. Good luck and have fun!

TRY THIS!

☐ Use ALL of the pieces you grabbed, no matter what they are.
☐ For extra kudos, use ONLY the random pieces you grabbed.

LEGO Language

Lowell sphere
(noun) *say* lohuhl sfear

A 4x4x4-**stud** sphere constructed using **SNOT** techniques (see page 258). The method can be adapted to create tubes and other shapes. It was developed by Bruce Lowell in 2002.

LURP
(noun) *say* lerp

LURP is an acronym that stands for Little Ugly Rock Piece, as opposed to a **BURP** (Big Ugly Rock Piece). It's a term used by **AFOL**s to describe rocklike LEGO **parts** that were common from the late nineties for about a decade.

PRO TECHNIQUE
LEGO MATHS

One of the best ways to strengthen a **studs**-up **brick** and **plate** model is to add vertical reinforcement. To do this you need to understand some basic LEGO maths. Most importantly, remember that a LEGO brick is three plates high and a 2-stud brick standing on its end is exactly five plates high.

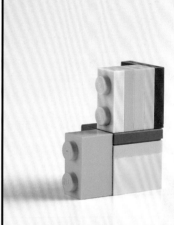

2 STUDS = 5 PLATES

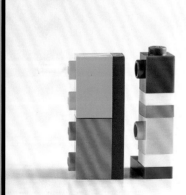

**4 STUDS =
2 ERLING BRICKS + 4 PLATES**

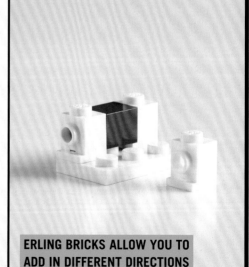

**ERLING BRICKS ALLOW YOU TO
ADD IN DIFFERENT DIRECTIONS**

PRO TECHNIQUE
LIGHTS

Adding lights to your LEGO models can really help bring them to life. LEGO makes a few lighting **elements**: there are some that come with **Powered UP**™ or **Power Functions** sets, or several regular LEGO sets come with small 2x3 light bricks.

The Powered UP or Power Functions lights are a bit more versatile as they are the same size as a **stud**, and the cables enable you to light up smaller or more specific areas. You can place different-coloured transparent **bricks** in front of them to change their colour; however, you do need to connect them via cables to a large battery box, which can take up a lot of room in a model.

Light bricks are much smaller and don't require cables, but unless you dismantle them and replace the batteries they only last a short period of time. You can build a switch to turn them on and off, or simply turn them on by pressing the button with your finger. They come in a limited range of colours. You can even create strobe effects by adding moving elements in front of the lights.

L

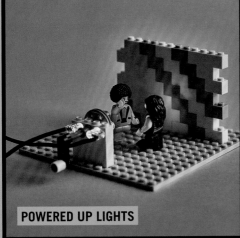

POWERED UP LIGHTS

LIGHT BRICKS

M is for...

MAGNETMOBILE

Magnetic forces are a fascinating phenomenon that you can easily play with. A fun trick is to place a magnet inside a LEGO® model, then use another magnet to move it around. Put the magnet low in the model and place the model on a table. Holding the other magnet in your fingers, put it beneath the table and use the magnetic force to drag the model along from below. You could make a vehicle that looks as though it is being driven around on a road, or make a beetle that will surprise people when it unexpectedly moves!

TRY THIS!

☐ Unless you're using very strong magnets, this works best with thin tables.

☐ Add a LEGO mechanism or handle to the magnet under the table to control the movement of the car.

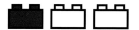

MAP

Make a mini build map of a familiar area: your house, your town, your neighbourhood, the park, or any place you know well and can map out. Put in any major features in **microscale** (see below) and include major roads, rivers and land features, such as mountain peaks, cliffs or valleys. You could make it a treasure map or a roadmap to show how to get from your house to school.

TRY THIS!

- ☐ **Baseplates** make a perfect start for a map.
- ☐ The bigger the area of your map, the smaller the features will be.
- ☐ You can look online for maps of your local area to help you.

LEGO Language

Macaroni
(noun) *say* makuhrohnee

A 2x2 quarter-round **brick** that resembles macaroni pasta, especially if it's yellow.

Microscale
(noun, adjective) *say* muykruhskayl

Any build that is smaller than **minifigure scale**. Examples of microscale are buildings that are only a few **bricks** high, vehicles that are only a few **studs** long, or trees that are just one cone. Basically, anything that makes a **minifigure** look like a giant is microscale.

MARS

What would you need for a mission to live on Mars? Make your own Mars base, and include ways to grow food, breathe air, generate power, get around the planet, do research, have fun and sleep. Make it as realistic or fantastic as you like: it's up to you!

TRY THIS!

- ☐ If you don't have lots of **parts** you can build it in **microscale**.
- ☐ Make some parts of the Mars base with removable roofs so that you can see inside.
- ☐ Build a Martian landscape for your base to sit on.
- ☐ How will you get to Mars? Make a rocket to take you there.

LEGO Language

Minidoll
(noun) *say* mineedol

The little doll-like figures that come with some sets such as LEGO Friends, Elves and Disney Princesses. Minidolls are very close to **minifigure scale** so you can swap **accessories** between the two quite easily.

Minifigure
(noun) *say* mineefiguh

The little LEGO people put together from pieces included in sets are called minifigures, so named because they are miniature action figures. It is often abbreviated to minifig.

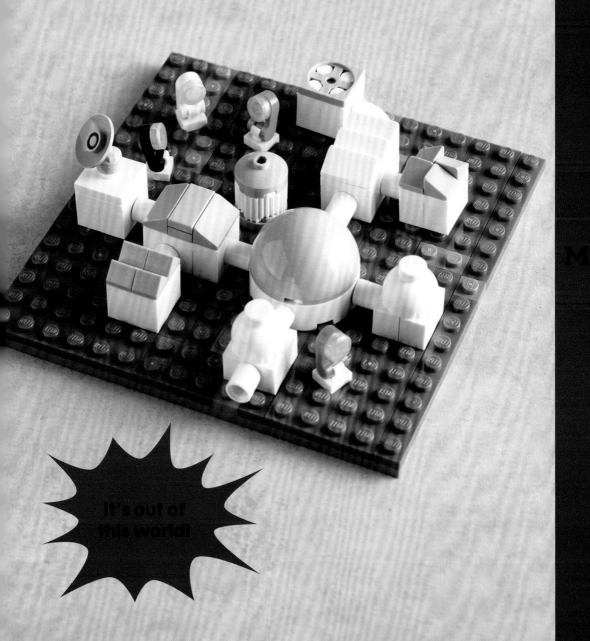

It's out of
this world!

MONSTER

You've probably made a LEGO monster before, but what about a monstrous version of an everyday object? Scare your **minifigures** with a monster fridge or a monster television, or chase them down the street with a monster car. Give your monster eyes, teeth, claws and wings; use crazy monster colours; and make it something unexpected — how would you fight a monster toaster?

TRY THIS!

☐ For an extra challenge, make your monster object a house.
☐ Make the monster colours contrast with the everyday object.

LEGO Language

Minifigure scale
(noun, adjective) *say* mineefiguh skayl

Any model, **diorama** or **accessory** that is scaled to be populated or used by **minifigures**.

MOC
(adjective) *say* mok

Acronym for My Own Creation. Refers to any fan-made build that is not an official LEGO set. We all love LEGO sets but sometimes it's fun to create a unique build. Usage: 'Your MOCs just keep getting better and better!'

module
(noun) *say* mojoohl

A module is a smaller component of a larger build. Sometimes a module can be separated from the larger build. This can be because the modules were built by different builders, or at different times, or to make it easier to move the larger build around.

177

MUSIC

Create your own musical instrument, either real or imagined, and start your own LEGO band. For an extra challenge you can try to make it actually produce sounds. For example, make shaking instruments filled with loose LEGO **tiles** or **plates**, or create a LEGO tea-chest (or washtub) bass.

TRY THIS!

☐ Musical instruments are often complex shapes, so you can use **SNOT** or **N.P.U.**

Give me a beat. And-a one, two, three, four ...

PRO TECHNIQUE MAPPING

Sometimes models are large and it's hard to figure out what structure and layout you need to even begin building it. A good way to work this out is to map it before you start, by drawing a plan on paper at a smaller scale or at full size. You can also do this digitally with a graphics program or even a LEGO building program such as LEGO digital design software (see pages 68–69). A good plan will help you iron out many of the problems and worries you might have before you build, saving you a lot of time and effort.

PLAN ON PAPER FIRST

N is for...

N

 **N**AME

Use your LEGO® **bricks** to make a nameplate for your door or desk. It could be built using **SNOT** (see page 258) or just as **brick-built** letters on large **plates**. You can use a few decorations that represent you and the things you like: add some flowers or **minifigs**!

TRY THIS!

- ☐ Use your favourite colours, or the colours of your favourite sports team.
- ☐ Uppercase letters are easier to build.
- ☐ LEGO has released a lot of cool curved and angled **tiles** you can use.

NARRATE

Ask a friend or family member to give you three story elements:
- a character name
- something that person wants
- something they're afraid of.

   Build a LEGO model that includes these three elements; for example, a character called Geraldine Gingerbread who really wants a magic sword, but is scared of pizza.

TRY THIS!

☐ Start with the thing your character wants and build a scene.
☐ Put the thing your character is scared of between them and the thing they want.
☐ Make your character's face express if they are scared or happy.

LEGO Language

Neo-Classic
(adjective) *say* neeohklasik

A term applied to LEGO models that seek to update a **Classic** LEGO set or theme using new LEGO **parts**, techniques or more modern aesthetics. An example was 'Neo-Classic Space', which sought to create updated versions of vintage Space LEGO sets.

N.P.U.
(adverb) *say* en-pee-yu

An **AFOL** initialism that stands for Nice Part Use. It describes an unexpected way to use a LEGO **element** in a model. Usage: 'Using pumpkins as segments of a caterpillar is N.P.U.'

Once upon a time ...

NECKLACE

Did you know you can create wearable LEGO models, such as necklaces and bracelets? Start by making a base: you can use LEGO string **parts** or LEGO DOTS® bands if you have them, or you could even build something from **clips** and **plates** that folds around your wrist or into a long chain that you can wear around your neck. Remember to make them loose enough so that they don't hurt and can easily slide off or clip apart for removal. Once you have the base, you can decorate it any way you like. Make a superhero emblem or a LEGO flower. Use bright colours and transparent pieces to give it some bling!

TRY THIS!

- ☐ Make sure your decorations are attached strongly, ideally by more than 1 **stud**.
- ☐ Use **tiles** or smooth **slopes** to make the piece more comfortable to wear.
- ☐ Create a whole wearable item of clothing, such as an armoured helmet or sparkly glove.

189

NIGHTLIGHT

Build a LEGO nightlight that fits over a lamp and creates interesting shadows. If there are particular shapes or colours you like, try to include those. You can make shapes using negative space, and coloured light with transparent **bricks** or panels.

TRY THIS!

- ☐ Make LEGO shapes to cast shadows, or make holes in LEGO walls to cast light patterns.
- ☐ Turn the model around the light to see the patterns move.
- ☐ If a lamp is too big, build over a torch or phone.

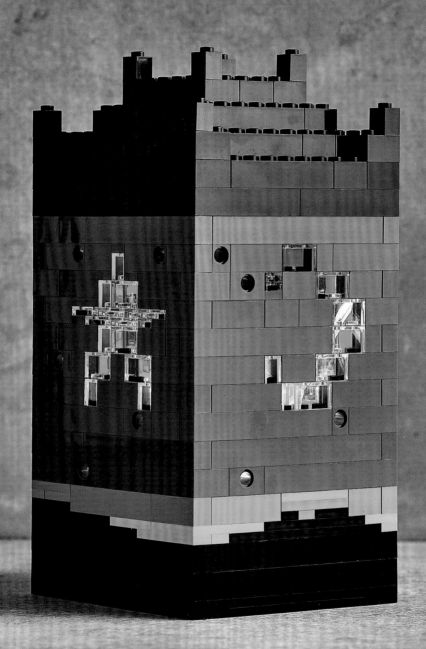

PRO TECHNIQUE
NEW

LEGO is releasing new **parts** and parts in new colours all the time. One of the most valuable things you can do as a LEGO builder is to keep an eye out for these. New parts often enable totally new ways to connect existing pieces, and can allow you to create shapes that were impossible before.

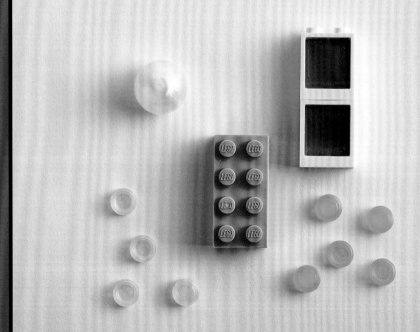

NEW OPALESCENT COLOURS

COOL NEW COLOURS

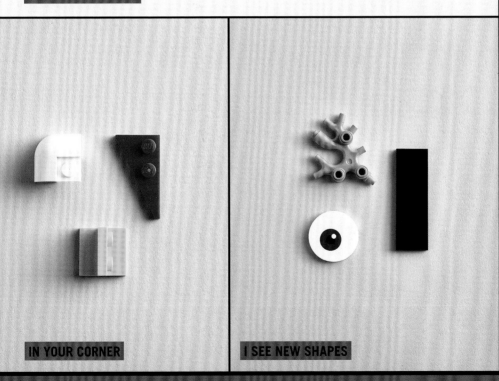

IN YOUR CORNER

I SEE NEW SHAPES

O is for...

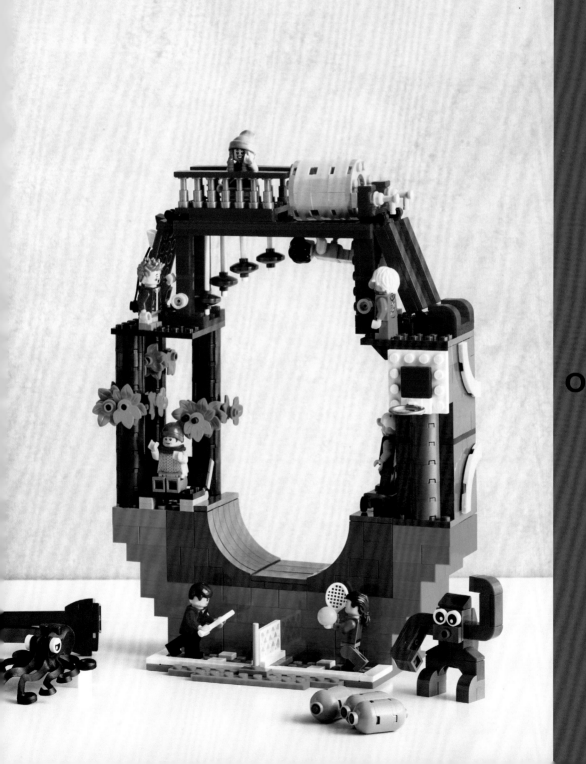

OBJECT

Have you ever looked really closely at everyday objects? Have you tried making one out of LEGO®? Pick something mundane and everyday that's an interesting shape and see how well you can reproduce it. You can change the scale and build bigger than life-size, which will allow you to make complex shapes more easily, but also try one at life-size to see if you can manage it.

TRY THIS!

- ☐ Start by getting the shape right. Don't worry about the colours at first.
- ☐ For an extra challenge, make your LEGO object work like the real thing!

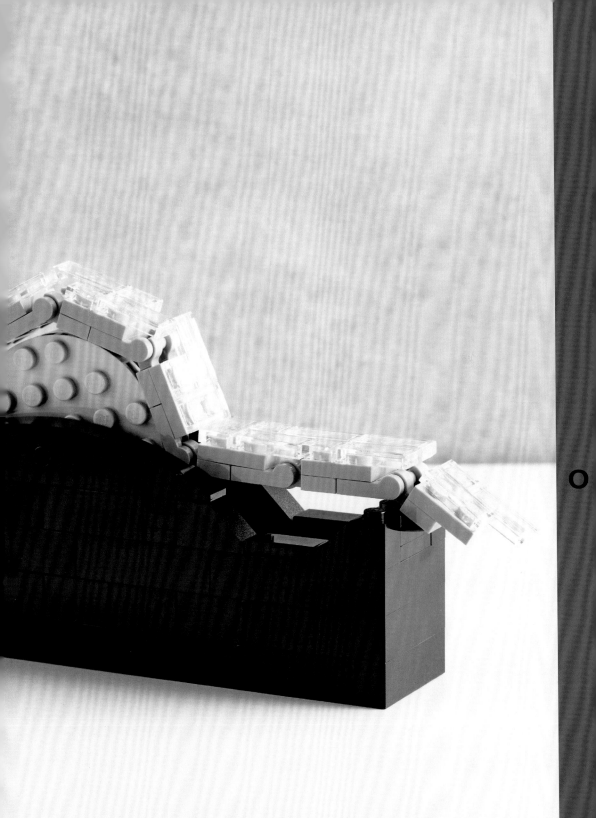

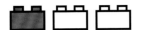

PPOSITE

Opposites are an interesting thing to try to create. Making a model that incorporates two opposing ideas in one build can be a fun challenge. Hot and cold, dark and light, big and small: whatever opposites you can think of, try to make a model that includes both. A good old-fashioned battle between good and bad would be fun to create. You might even consider making the opposite of yourself!

TRY THIS!

☐ Tell a story with your opposites: why are the two opposite things together in the same place?

☐ What happens when your opposites touch or meet? Does fire melt the ice, or does the ice put the fire out?

O

LEGO Language

Orient Expedition
(proper noun) *say* awreeuhnt ekspuhdishuhn

This was the name of LEGO's 2003 follow-up to the Adventurers line from the late 1990s. It featured the return of their hero **minifig**, Johnny Thunder, with the magnificently named Lord Sam Sinister as the villain. It is notable for being the first, and only, LEGO **System** range (not including **DUPLO**®) to include elephants, up until new moulded elephants were introduced in 2021.

PRO TECHNIQUE
ORGANISE

Being organised will help you streamline your building process. When you know exactly where the **part** you need is, it can drastically cut down the time it takes for you to fetch it for your build. Most people just have a big tub of LEGO that they tip on the floor and sift through. But if you have time and patience to separate your LEGO into groups, it can save you time looking for that needle in the haystack.

This can be as basic as separating types of parts into different containers, or as complex as storing each part in each different colour in their own little drawers. You can separate it into **bricks**, **plates**, panels, glass, **minifigures**, utensils and weapons, special bits, **clips** and **bars**, **wheels**, wings, **wedges**, **slopes** and any other categories you like.

Some people prefer to separate their pieces by colour, but Brickman finds it much easier to find a red 2x2 in a tub of multicoloured 2x2 bricks than a red 2x2 in a tub of red bricks. Ultimately, though, it is up to you as to how you do it, as long as you know how it's done.

O

P is for...

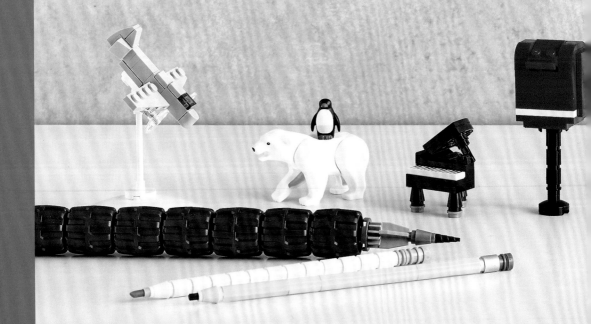

P

PALACE

Build a LEGO® palace fit for a prince or princess. It could be as big as a castle, or as small as you can build. Include a place to hang a crown, and decorate it inside and out with bright colours and interesting shapes. Use a **minifigure** prince or princess, or make a **brick-built** one and build the palace to scale.

TRY THIS!

☐ Make the back of your palace open so you can see the rooms inside, or have the front of it hinge open like a doll's house.

☐ What kind of rooms do royals need? Include a throne room, a banquet hall, and don't forget the kitchen and bathroom.

PET

Build a pet in any scale you like. It can be a real pet, or an imaginary animal. Think about what your pet likes to eat and do, and make sure they have everything they need. Focus on the animal's features: long tail, blue eyes or shaggy fur.

TRY THIS!

- ☐ Build a carrying case for your LEGO pet, with a door, windows and air vents.
- ☐ LEGO has released many **minifig-scale** animals: pick one and build it a home. Don't forget to include somewhere for it to sleep.

LEGO Language

Palisade
(noun) *say* paluhsayd

LEGO **bricks**, either 1x2 or 1x4, on which the sides and corners aren't flat, but bulge out to give the illusion of a row of rounded bricks. Originally used to create the palisade-style wooden walls of Wild West and Castle sets. *Also known as*: logs, puffy brick.

Paradisa
(proper noun) *say* pahrah'deezah

Paradisa was a range of LEGO Town sets that was produced between 1992 and 1997, focusing on an idyllic beach holiday setting. These sets included houses, beaches and shops in shades of white and pink surrounded by LEGO palm trees. Paradise indeed!

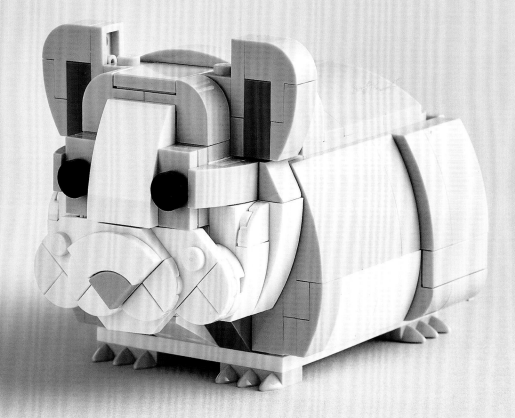

P

PLANET

Have you ever wondered what other planets would look like? Would they have giant purple rocks? Six moons? What kind of life would exist there? Would the trees have tentacles and the grass be blue? Grab a big LEGO **baseplate** and try to build another world, making it as weird and wonderful as you can! LEGO has leaves and plant pieces in lots of different colours, but don't be afraid to use LEGO pieces in different ways: try making a plant made out of **minifig** hairpieces, for example!

TRY THIS!

- ☐ Does your planet have intelligent life? Include an example.
- ☐ Add homes or vehicles, but make sure they suit the crazy world you've built!
- ☐ Add some minifig explorers to interact with the inhabitants of the planet.

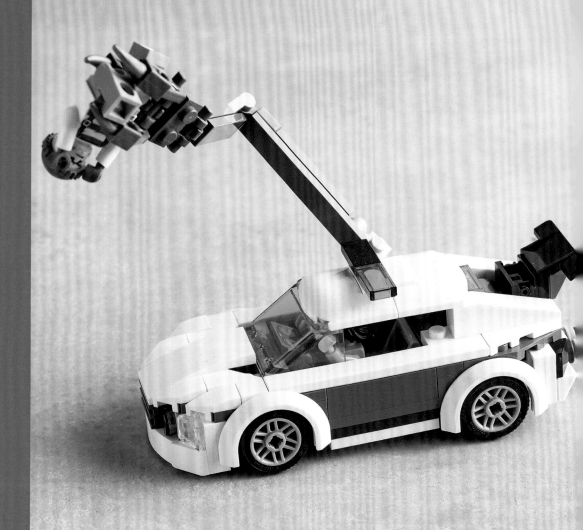

POLICE

Build the ultimate LEGO police vehicle. It could be a super-fast car or a helicopter. Make sure it has red and blue lights, room for a driver, plus a cool way to catch and lock up the criminals.

Your police vehicle doesn't have to be a regular car or bike. It could be a giant robot piloted by a police officer, or a magical horse-drawn carriage driven by fairy police!

TRY THIS!

☐ Place the vehicle in a **diorama** showing the whole crime scene.
☐ Make an undercover vehicle with pop-out lights and features.
☐ Add an extension for transporting captured criminals to gaol.
☐ What would happen if the criminals stole your super police vehicle and used it for evil?

P

LEGO Language

Part
(noun) *say* paht

Any piece made by LEGO. It could be a **brick**, **plate**, **wheel**, axle, **minifig wig**, flag or flower.

Parts monkey
(noun) *say* pahts mungkee

A LEGO builder who takes a special interest in individual LEGO **elements**. A parts monkey views most LEGO sets as **part**s packs for their collections to either sort or build with.

POP-UP

Create a LEGO model which opens and folds out like a pop-up book. Start with two large **plates** the same size for the front and back of your book, then create a spine, the same length as the plates, but about a quarter of the width. Link all three pieces with at least two **hinges** so that you can fold them up into a book, with the hinged part becoming the spine. Then use hinges, ball **joints** or **Technic™ connector pegs** to mount sections of a **diorama** that can fold flat when the book's covers come together, and pop up when the book is opened.

TRY THIS!

- ☐ Pop-ups can be as simple as a single piece that is pulled up.
- ☐ Have a look at real pop-up books for inspiration.

LEGO Language

Plate
(noun) *say* playt

A core LEGO **part** that is one-third the height of a **brick** and has at least one **stud** on top. When five plates are stacked sideways they are the same width as a 2-stud piece. Plates don't have to be square or rectangular: there are also round plates and **wedge** plates. *Also known as*: flats. *See also*: LEGO maths (page 166).

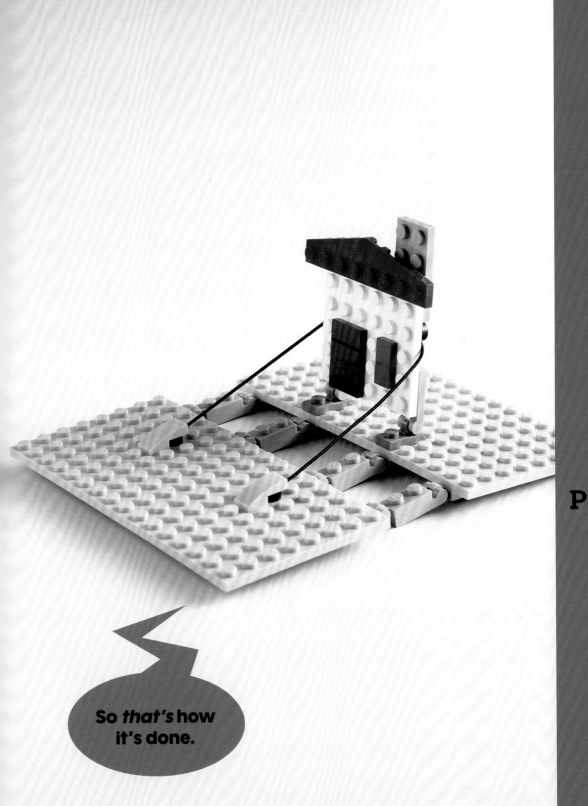

So *that's* how it's done.

Portraits

Create LEGO versions of your family and friends. This could be as simple as making **minifig** versions of them, or as complex as building their faces as LEGO mosaics, or even 3D faces! Add special touches to the portrait to surprise your subject with your creative artwork. Focus on the main features: does the person have long or short hair? A round face or a pointy chin?

TRY THIS!

☐ For more of a challenge, produce portraits of your favourite sporting team or a popular superhero, or even a music band (with their instruments).

LEGO Language

Powered UP™, Power Functions
(proper noun) *say* powuhd up, powuh fungkshuhnz

Power Functions is a system of electric components, mainly used in **Technic** sets. It includes motors and lights (see page 167) to enhance your builds. As of 2021, Power Functions has largely been replaced by Powered UP, with smart motors and app-based controls.

Purist
(noun) *say* pyoohrist

This is what we call a LEGO builder who does not use any customisations, such as cut, painted or otherwise modified parts, decals, or custom accessories that are made by companies other than LEGO.

P

PRESENT

If there is a special day coming up, such as a birthday, holiday, wedding or festival, why not make a decorative gift box with a lid to contain a present? Try to think of something representative of the special day and build it in colours associated with it. For example, for a person's birthday, think of their favourite colours and things they like and decorate it to match, or for Christmas you could make it in festive red and green. You can build it as fancy as you like, so if you have any special pieces in transparent or metallic colours you could incorporate those.

TRY THIS!

☐ For extra excitement, add a pop-up mechanism to the gift, like the jack-in-the-box on pages 132–133.
☐ What about using a secret locking mechanism with a key (see pages 148–149) so the recipient can keep their treasures in the box afterwards?

PRO TECHNIQUE
PERSPECTIVE

If you don't have lots of LEGO or only limited space in which to build, then using a technique called 'forced perspective' can help make your small LEGO creations feel much bigger. By building a scene in layers, with large scale at the front and small scale at the back, you can give your small model the illusion of being much deeper than it actually is.

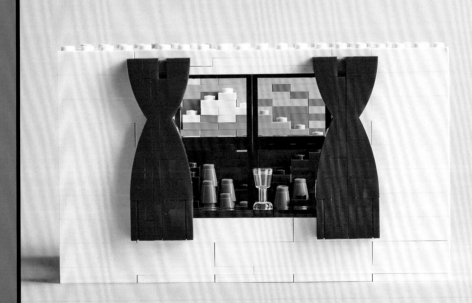

DISTANT MOUNTAINS

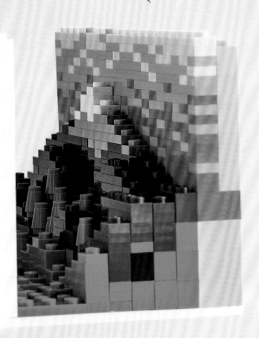

FORCED PERSPECTIVE

P

Q is for...

QUEEN

Use LEGO® to build the queen of a fantasy realm, the queen of a beehive, the queen of the fairies, the Queen of England, the evil queen from a fairytale, the queen of the suburbs, a queen for a chess game, or the queen of an alien planet. Give her an appropriate outfit, a crown and a throne. She can be graceful and regal, kind and just, or a scheming sorceress looking to get all the riches and power through evil means.

TRY THIS!

☐ Make sure your queen looks powerful: standing tall and strong.
☐ Her crown should stand out in a bright colour, or with special **parts**.
☐ Build her an elaborate throne that shows her power.

I'm the queen of the castle ...

QUEUE

When there is an event that people are excited to attend and experience for themselves, they inevitably end up in a long queue waiting to go in. Use **minifigures** to create a queue for an event that you might stand in line for, such as a concert, the theatre, an art exhibition, a circus, sports event or some other kind of amazing show that you and your minifigures would love. Use minifig **accessories** to show the clothes they might wear to the event; for example, if it's a sporting event, they could dress in team colours.

TRY THIS!

☐ Start with something you know you'd love to go to.
☐ For a harder build, get someone else to decide what people would queue up to see or do, then build it.

LEGO Language

Q bricks
(noun) *say* kyooh briks

A Q brick is a term used by LEGO and Brickman to identify a **brick** or **element** that is a rare or out-of-production piece. Usage: 'Don't use all of my Q bricks in your model, they're precious pieces.'

QUATRO
(proper noun) *say* kwotroh

QUATRO is the name of a range of LEGO sets produced from 2004 to 2006 for babies and toddlers aged one to three years, featuring bricks similar to **DUPLO**®, but four times the size of regular LEGO bricks.

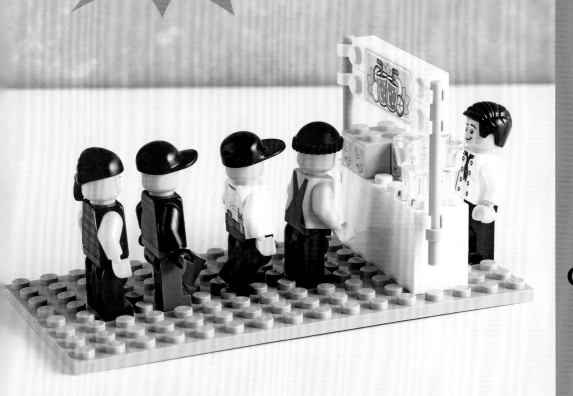

The last four letters of 'queue' aren't silent, they're just waiting their turn.

Q

QUICK

A fun way to make any project more of a challenge is to give yourself a time limit to build it. Seeing what you can build within a set timeframe can be a great way to exercise your creativity. Then try shorter time limits and see what you can produce there. If you find that you can't finish anything in the time limits you set, you might try to simplify your ideas and construction and find quicker ways of achieving the same thing. Try some of these ideas: give yourself 5 minutes to build a house or garden; try 10 minutes for a car or an animal; or 15 minutes to build a castle or an aeroplane. A time limit for any project should keep you on track and help you to make design decisions quickly.

TRY THIS!

- ☐ Don't be hard on yourself! Start with simple ideas and generous time limits, then slowly work up to more complex ideas and shorter time limits.
- ☐ Use repeatable **modules** and big **parts** to save time, as in the ice castle shown here.

PRO TECHNIQUE
QUANTITY

'Working within your means' is a great piece of advice for any artist and, unless you have your own personal brick pit, you'll need to make do with the amount of LEGO you already have. When you get ready to start building a new project, it's a good idea to make sure you have enough of the bits and pieces you'll need; for example, if you're making a large purple castle, but you don't actually have much purple or castle-specific pieces, you might find it hard. Gather all the pieces you are likely to use for your project and get an idea of the scope of the build. This will save you from the heartache of realising part way through that you might not be able to finish it.

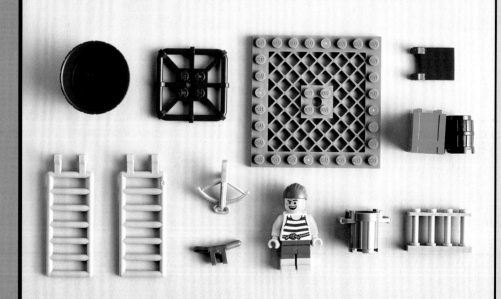

MAKE SURE YOU HAVE ALL YOU NEED

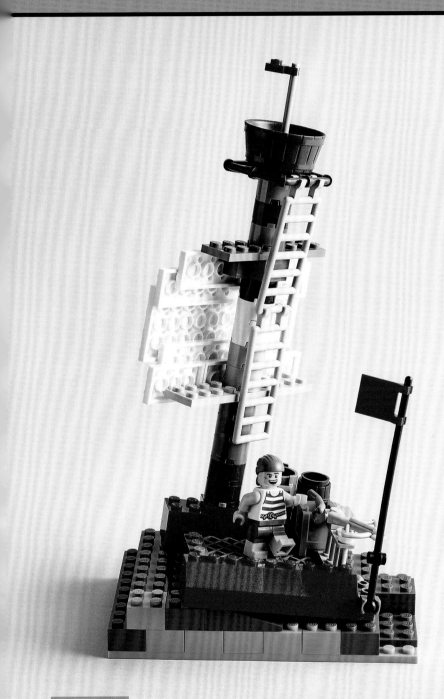

AHOY THERE!

Q

R is for...

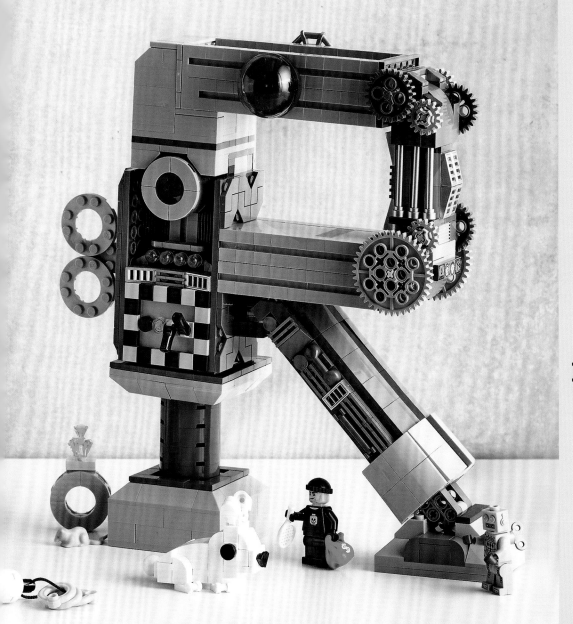

R

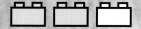

Racetrack

Build a racing track or series of obstacles for your toy cars to race through! If you don't have the space or **bricks** to build a whole racetrack, you can just build the important features, such as the start and finish lines, signs telling you which way the cars need to go, and obstacles for the car to navigate, such as oil slicks, jumps or rings of fire. Now build a LEGO® racing car (see page 234) to drive on it.

TRY THIS!

- You can add moving obstacles to your course, such as a wrecking ball that swings across the track.
- Bring your track to life with novelty obstacles, such as a shark tank or 'bottomless' pit.

Ready, set, go!

R

233

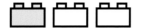

RACING CAR

Build your own LEGO racing car. Look at a real racing car for inspiration: does it have a big spoiler at the back? Does it have just four wheels or does it have more? Don't forget to add a steering wheel and a **minifig** to drive it. Build it with lots of **broomability**! Make a LEGO racetrack (see page 232) to drive it on, with lots of obstacles for the car to avoid.

TRY THIS!

- [ ] Make your car in a bright colour to stand out and decorate it with stripes or patterns.
- [ ] The fastest cars are low and very smooth, so use **tiles** to make your car sleek and mount your **wheels** so that the car rides close to the ground, but doesn't touch it.

LEGO Language

Rainbow warrior
(noun) *say* raynboh woreeuh

The type of multicoloured LEGO creations that we all build when we're little, or when we don't have lots of **parts** in the same colours.

Res-Q
(proper noun) *say* reskyooh

Res-Q was a short-lived line of LEGO Town sets that ran through 1998 and 1999. It featured black-and-yellow vehicles with transparent blue windscreens, rescuing **minifigs**.

R

**Red cars
go faster.**

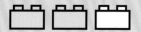

RECYCLE

Build a small LEGO model, between 10 cm (4 inches) and 20 cm (8 inches) in size, of anything you like. (If you already have a model, or LEGO set, of that size that you're willing to pull apart, then start with that instead.) Then pull it apart and challenge yourself to use ONLY those same pieces to build something new.

TRY THIS!

- [ ] Make the two models completely different from each other: turn a house into a rocket.
- [ ] This is a chance for some **N.P.U.**, such as turning **parts** sideways or upside down.

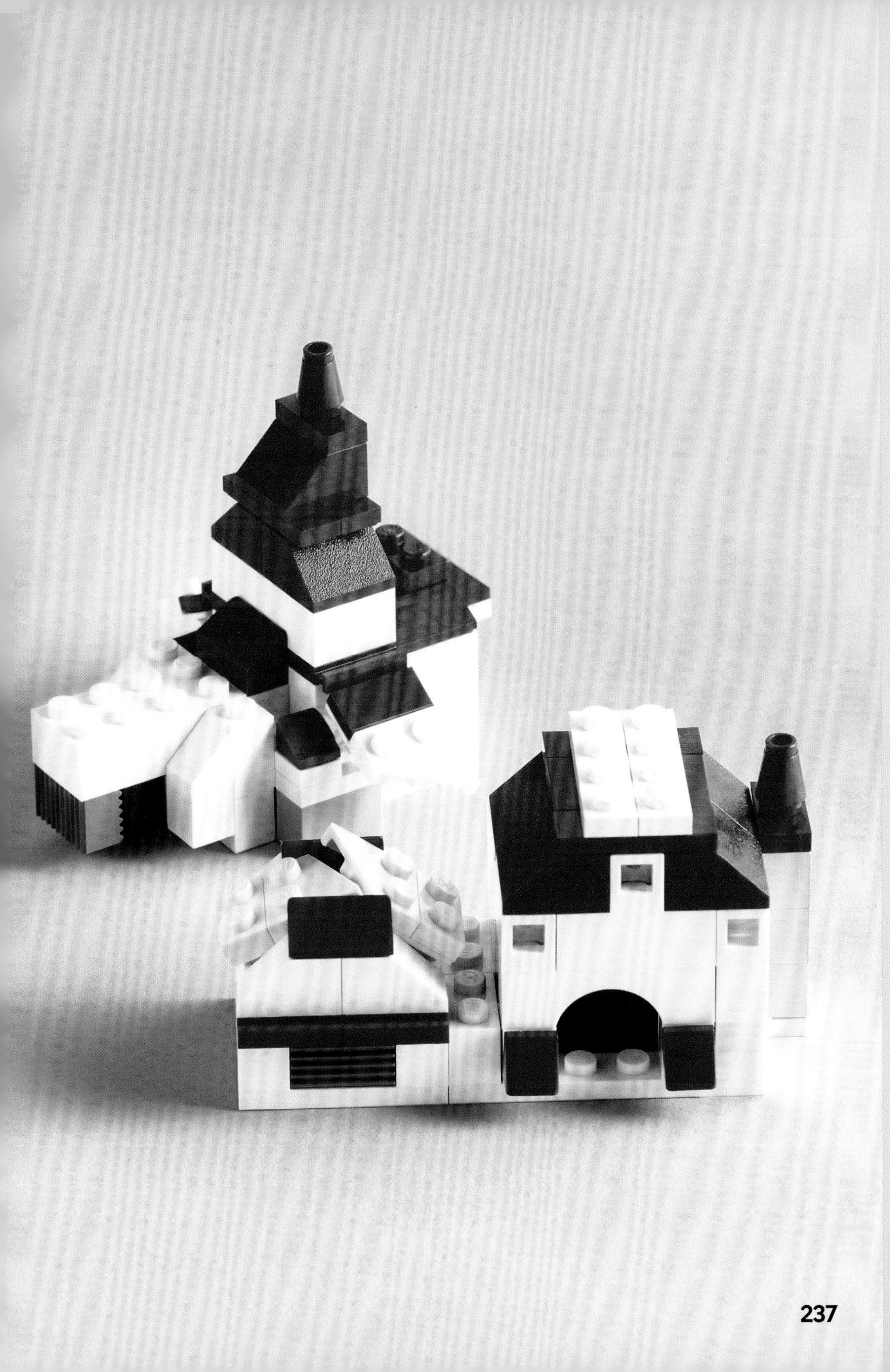

R

RESCUE

Create a LEGO rescue vehicle to save people from dangerous situations. It could be a lifeguard's jet ski, a helicopter with a harness or a special truck with inflatable side barriers to stop out-of-control hotdog vans!

TRY THIS!

☐ Make sure your rescue vehicle is brightly coloured and has lights or sirens so that <u>minifigs</u> know it's coming to save them.

☐ Fire engines, ambulances and police cars are rescue vehicles.

LEGO Language

Roof tile
(noun) *say* roohf tuyl

This is the part name for straight <u>slope bricks</u>, as they were originally used to create sloping roofs on house models. They come in a huge variety of sizes and colours now, with many being printed and used as control panels and dashboards in vehicles. *Also known as*: slopes, cash registers; when inverted: upside down slopes.

Round bricks
(noun) *say* rownd briks

LEGO <u>elements</u> with a circular, or semicircular, shape. There are 1x1, 2x2 and 4x4 round <u>bricks</u>, as well as square 2x2 bricks which have a rounded top. For larger circles there are semicircle 4x8 bricks and quarter-circle 4x4 bricks. Sometimes these bricks have nicknames such as barrels, cans, tubes, cylinders, engines or mailboxes.

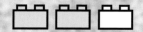

ROBOT

Imagine robot versions of different animals and appliances: what would a robot toaster look like? Or a robot fish? Choose something you know well from around the house or something you can look up and find lots of pictures of. Then try to imagine what a robotic version of that thing would look like. Would it have buttons? Would it have exhaust pipes from its engine or an antenna so it could be controlled remotely? Would it have wheels or propellers to make it move instead of legs and wings? You could try drawing it first to get the idea right before you build it.

TRY THIS!

- Robots needn't be grey: add colour!
- Most robots have some way of moving: try legs, wings, **wheel**s or treads.

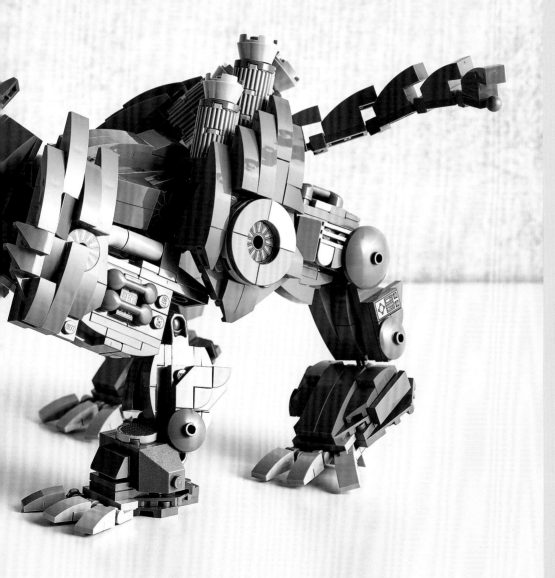

PRO TECHNIQUE
RAILS

Do you have any LEGO trains or train tracks? Did you ever think about using train tracks as structural **elements** to help support something? Well, you can. You can even use the curved track pieces to make giant circles or curves that would normally take tons of small LEGO **hinges** to create. Try it out on your next creation and see how you can use them.

SPACE STATION

R

S is for...

S

Scale

A lot of the time, things you would like to build in LEGO® are too big to build at their real size, so you need to change the scale to make the model achievable. Changing the scale of an object is a fun way to replicate it. When scaling something down from large to small, focus on the basic shapes and features of the subject, and don't worry about tiny details. But you can also take something that's usually really small and scale it up. Try making a supersized insect or a giant pencil. As shown opposite, you could try making one object at many different scales: one tiny, one at normal size and one larger than normal.

TRY THIS!

☐ Start by writing down the main details that will make the model recognisable; for example, yellow colour, orange beak, tail, eye.

LEGO Language

Slope bricks
(noun) *say* slohp briks

Any **brick** that has a vertically angled section that tapers in or out from the base. Some are sharp angles, some are gentle slopes. These were originally **roof tiles**, created to make sloping roofs for houses. *Also known as*: pyramid bits.

It's a
quack-up!

S

SECRET

For a fun and sneaky project, build a model with a hidden compartment, such as a secret drawer, a hidden door or a camouflaged plug. Make it big enough to stash a small treasure or a keepsake. Just don't forget it's there!

TRY THIS!

- ☐ The door of the secret compartment should be easy to open, but hard to see.
- ☐ Make the model look like something else, such as a coffee cup or a train, so that no one suspects something is hidden inside.

LEGO Language

S.N.I.R.
(noun) *say* es-en-uy-ah

An initialism for Studs Not In Row. These are pieces that have **studs** that are not aligned to the regular LEGO grid. They are usually halfway between regular stud positions or centred in place of four studs in a square. Common examples are **jumper plates**, which are usually 1x2 and 2x2 **plates** with a centred stud.

SNOT
(noun) *say* snot

An acronym that stands for Studs Not On Top. These are **bricks** or **plates** that have **studs** on the sides of the brick as well as (or instead of) on the top. They are used to change the build angle and increase the available building surfaces. They can also be **brackets**. *See also* the Pro Technique on page 258.

SIDEWAYS

You've built things the right way up and upside down, but have you tried building something sideways? Instead of the object being built from the bottom up, start at one side and place all your **bricks** facing the other side. The bricks are sideways, but the model is still the right side up!

TRY THIS!

☐ Draw a picture of what you want to build, but then turn the picture sideways to help you see what it will look like as you build it up.

☐ Building sideways means some LEGO **parts** will look different, and is a good time to try some **N.P.U.**

LEGO Language

SNOT-built
(adjective)
say snot-bilt

Refers to a section of LEGO that is built onto **SNOT bricks**. Usage: 'The front part of the truck is a SNOT-built extension.'

SNOT lettering
(noun) *say* snot letuhring

Refers to words and letters made of LEGO that use SNOT bricks to hold the component pieces in place.

S

SIGN

Make a sign for your room. You can either create the letters from regular **bricks** or use **SNOT lettering**. It could be your name, or a warning sign: 'Private. Keep out.' Use removable adhesive pads to stick it to your wall, or use string to hang it from a doorhandle.

TRY THIS!

- ☐ Do you have a LEGO room or somewhere you like to build your LEGO? Add a sign like 'LEGOratory' or 'Builder at work'.
- ☐ Make arrow signs to set up a treasure-hunt trail in your yard.

S

Put your name
on the door to show
everyone who's boss.

SILHOUETTE

This project is all about shadows. Shine a bright light on an object placed in front of a large piece of drawing paper, and trace the outline of the shadow. You can trace the profile of a person or a distinctive object such as a saucepan or a vase. Use this traced silhouette as a template to construct the outline from LEGO and then fill in the middle to make it solid. Once it's finished, display it and see if people can recognise who or what it represents.

TRY THIS!

☐ All you need to worry about is the shape, so use any colour.

LEGO Language

Splooshability
(adjective) *say* sploohsh-uhbiluhtee

An evaluation of how well a model can be picked up and moved around in water to simulate floating or submerged motion. A small, sturdy boat has high splooshability, whereas a corner shop has low splooshability. *See also* **swooshability** and **broomability**.

Stud
(noun) *say* stud

LEGO's ingenious system to hold **bricks** together uses circular protrusions on top of the brick, called studs, to slot into spaces of equal size in the bottom of the brick, called **anti-studs**. All studs have 'LEGO' printed on them. *Also known as*: dots, knobs, buttons.

S

255

STAINED GLASS

Transparent **bricks** are some of the nicest decorative bricks available to build with. They come in lots of awesome colours and some of them even glitter. Using mainly transparent bricks will make a model that catches the sunlight and looks awesome on a windowsill or hanging in a window.

TRY THIS!

☐ There aren't many big transparent bricks or **plates**, so it may be easier to start building your stained glass model on a long non-transparent brick, then lock all of the stacked pieces with another long plate or brick across the top.

LEGO Language

Swooshability
(adjective) *say* swoohsh-uhbiluhtee

An evaluation of how well a model can be picked up and moved around to simulate flight. A small, sturdy aeroplane has high swooshability, whereas an octopus has low swooshability. *See also* **splooshability** and **broomability**.

System
(noun) *say* sistuhm

The name given to LEGO's 'regular' brick-based construction method; that is, all LEGO **elements** fitting together in many ways for many different builds. LEGO's other construction systems include **Technic**™ and **DUPLO**®.

PRO TECHNIQUE
SNOT BUILDING

SNOT **bricks** are bricks that have **studs** on the sides as well as (or instead of) the top, and they are extremely useful for making complex LEGO models. Side studs not only allow you to add details such as flat **plates** to decorate your models, but also whole other structures built sideways onto the regular stacked bricks. You can even use a SNOT brick on another SNOT brick and have the studs going upside down! SNOT bricks allow you to add onto your construction in any direction you like, increasing the complexity and detail.

MAKE SPHERES WITH STUDS IN ALL DIRECTIONS

SNOT BRICKS ALLOW DETAILS
TO BE ADDED ON THE SIDES

DECORATE WITH PLATES

S

259

T is for...

TINY

Build a tiny version of a big thing using LEGO®. What's the biggest thing you can think of? A skyscraper? A jumbo jet? Try to make one as small as you can from LEGO **parts**, but make sure it's recognisable as what it is supposed to be.

TRY THIS!

☐ Find LEGO parts that represent the big thing's main shapes; e.g. **wedge plates** for plane wings; 1x1 round plates for wheels.

☐ **Minifig** rollerskates make great wheels for tiny vehicles.

LEGO Language

Tablescrap
(noun) *say* taybuhlskrap

A small, clever LEGO build that doesn't stand alone as a completed creation. A tablescrap may be a simple exploration of a technique (such as an interesting way to combine several **elements** to make an odd shape) or it may be a recognisable item that's just too small to merit presentation on its own. Many LEGO builders save their tablescraps for use in future creations. From 'table scraps'; that is, leftovers.

Technic™
(proper noun) *say* teknik

LEGO Technic is one of the core ranges for older kids, but many of its basic components, such as pegs and beams, have become common in a lot of other LEGO sets. Technic has robust **connections** and makes it easy to add moving parts.

It's amazing how much detail you can put into a tiny build.

TOTEM POLE

Build a stack of LEGO objects, animals or people. You can make them as complex or simple as you like: a frowning mask, an eagle with wings, a flower, a robot, a turtle, or anything you like.

TRY THIS!

☐ You don't have to build everything at once: concentrate on building each part separately. Just make sure that they all have ways to be connected on top of each other.

LEGO Language

Thill for gig
(noun) *say* thil fuh gig

LEGO's name for the LEGO **part** (#2397) originally used as a horse hitch. It might sound Danish, but it is in fact English! A 'thill' is an old English word for the shafts that attach an animal to a cart or carriage, and a gig is another word for a cart or small horse-drawn carriage, which is literally what the part was designed for.

Tile
(noun) *say* tuyl

A **plate** with a smooth top, useful for creating a flat surface on a build. Tiles can be rectangular, square, round or other shapes. Some tiles have stickers that turn them into specific items, such as a stop sign or a pizza.

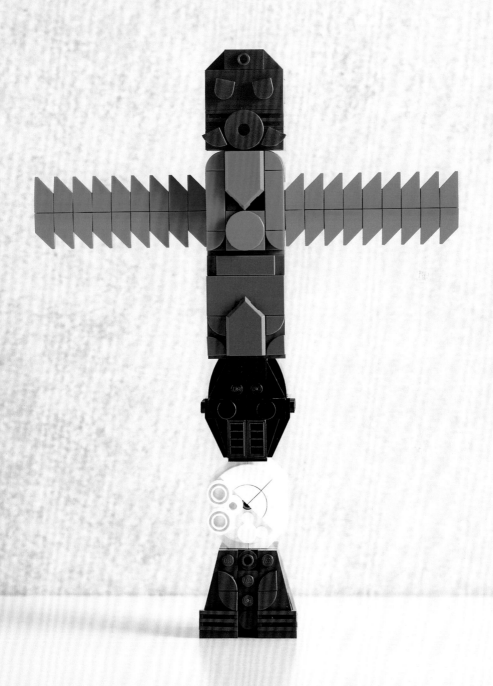

TRAIN

Build a LEGO train. It could be any kind of train you know or like: a steam train or a super-fast bullet train. If you don't have train wheels, any **wheels** or round plates will do.

TRY THIS!

- [ ] For a bigger challenge, try building extra carriages and a caboose.
- [ ] You don't need LEGO train track **parts**: build your own rails with **plates** and **tiles** or just roll the train on the floor.

T

TREEHOUSE

Make your dream house, but put it in a tree! Building LEGO trees can be tricky, so make sure you build yours nice and strong before you start adding the house. Use **SNOT**, **Technic** or overlapping **bricks** to give the tree a solid trunk. And make sure it's stuck down to a **baseplate** or has a wide base so that it balances (see pages 38–39) when you start adding floors. Remember your **minifigs** will need a way to climb up into the treehouse (and maybe make a quick escape if needed!) You don't have to use LEGO leaves if you don't have many: try using green **plates** or bricks. Or you could make it an autumn tree with reds, yellows and oranges.

TRY THIS!

- [ ] Using SNOT to add vertical LEGO plates to your tree trunk can not only help strengthen the trunk, but add texture.
- [ ] Ball **joints** or **clip hinges** are a great way to make your tree's branches look more organic.

LEGO Language

Travis brick
(noun) *say* travuhs brik

A 1x1 LEGO brick with **studs** on four sides. Named for Travis Kunce, an **AFOL** who was known for his enthusiasm for the piece. A piece often used in SNOT building (see page 258). *Also known as*: SNOT cube, **knob stone**.

T

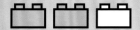

TYRES

Did you know that LEGO is the biggest tyre manufacturer in the world? Build something that uses tyres, but not as wheels! Think about other round shapes in nature and see if you can use tyres or wheels to represent them in a build. It's great **N.P.U.**

TRY THIS!

☐ You don't have to keep the tyres on their **wheel** hubs if you don't want to, but the wheel hubs will give you easy ways to connect the tyres to a model.

PRO TECHNIQUE
TEXTURE

By using LEGO **parts** in different directions or combinations, you can add texture to your models. Leaving LEGO **studs** exposed gives the illusion of rough, natural surfaces, whereas smooth **slopes**, curves, **tiles** and **SNOT** building (see page 258) make something look sleek and new. Using LEGO to create texture is best done by contrasting different areas: you need both smooth and rough textures in a model to highlight their differences.

ROUGH STONE

SLEEK ROCKET

T

U is for...

U

UFO

The future is now and everyone thought there would be flying cars. They haven't turned up yet, but until then we have to use our imaginations! Build a futuristic flying craft that uses some amazing made-up technology as a way of hovering above the ground.

TRY THIS!

- [ ] Don't forget to include a driver!
- [ ] What makes it go? Is it propelled by a jet engine, or a flying robot llama?
- [ ] Make your model look like it's flying by attaching clear LEGO® underneath.

U

UNDERNEATH

An interesting challenge is to build a model that appears to be crossing through the surface it is sitting on, such as a table. To achieve this, you would make two parts of the same thing: half of it above the surface and half of it below. Think of the surface as being a border between two different areas; for example, the surface of the ocean — the threshold between the sky and the water — or ground level, and what's happening underground. You can attach the bottom half of the model to the underside of a table with removable adhesive pads. Alternatively, just build the model as a **vignette**.

TRY THIS!

☐ Keep the thickness of the table in mind: you don't have to build the part of the model that would exist inside the table.

LEGO Language

Unitron
(proper noun) *say yoohnuhtron*

Unitron is the name of one of LEGO's space themes that ran from 1994 to 1995. It featured black and grey vehicles with neon green highlights and dark blue transparent windscreens. It is famous for being the last LEGO range to use the rare monorail system.

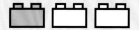

UNDERWATER

Even though most of our planet's surface is water, we haven't yet explored much of the ocean and there is a lot going on under the sea. So build yourself an underwater scene: it could be a research base for **minifigures**, the lost city of Atlantis, a haven for mermaids, a coral reef, a fish-person village, or an octopus's garden.

TRY THIS!

☐ Build a watery background (see pages 306–307) with a wall of stacked blue **bricks** or **SNOT-built** blue **plates**.

☐ Use clear **elements** to make it look like fish and other creatures are swimming in the sea.

UNICORNS

One mythical creature that captures our imaginations again and again is the unicorn, because it epitomises beauty and power. Make your own unicorn out of LEGO, but give it a special twist. Mix it up with something else that you like: what about a peppermint choc-chip ice-cream unicorn, or a retro silver spaceship unicorn with lightning racing stripes? The possibilities are endless, so you may need a special unicorn forest to keep them all in.

TRY THIS!

☐ The most important feature of a unicorn is its horn, so start there and see if you can find a way to make yours relate to your extra-crazy theme; for example, if you're making a racing robot unicorn, then its horn could be an exhaust pipe!

Have you ever seen a unicorn?

U

281

UPSIDE DOWN

Sometimes looking at an object from a different perspective can help you to see things you might not have noticed before. So building models in a different way can give you a new appreciation of ways to make something. Let's flip the script and build something upside down! You would usually build with the **studs** on the top, so try turning the LEGO **parts** so you're building with the studs on the bottom. As you can see here, you aren't building a normal model flipped on its head – you're using the *pieces* upside down to make something the right way up. Building upside down is a good skill to use to make detailed, interesting shapes that aren't possible with the normal way of building. These models show a combination of upside-down and normally oriented **bricks**.

TRY THIS!

- [ ] Start with something simple and familiar to get the hang of it.
- [ ] Some parts have inverted versions (such as **slopes** and **brackets**), which will make things a bit easier.

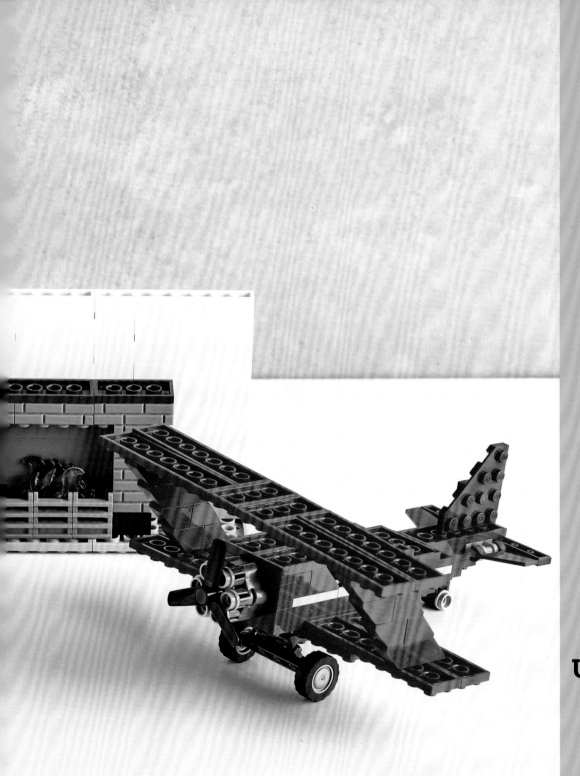

U

PRO TECHNIQUE
UP

Once you have completed a LEGO model and want to show it off, it can be as simple as plonking it on a flat surface — which is fine for a car, a house, a character or anything that should be on the ground. But when it comes to displaying a model that flies, floats through the air or zips through outer space, it can be fun to try and display it lifted up off the ground. You could make a stand for it, or prop it up with transparent clear **bricks**. Or you could try hanging it from the ceiling with wires — but if you haven't done this before, it's best to consult an adult who has (even if you are an adult).

CLEAR ELEMENTS MAKE IT FLY

How high
can you go?

UP, UP AND AWAY

V is for...

VENOM

Build something that has a poisonous feature. It could be a venomous snake, a stinging scorpion, a spotty toxic mushroom, or even a furry platypus (they have a poisonous spur on their hind feet).

TRY THIS!

- [ ] Most venomous things have sharp fangs or stingers, so add LEGO® teeth, horns or even swords.
- [ ] Bring your creation to life in a **vignette** with creatures or people running away.

Hissssssssssssss.

VILLAGE

Make a village from LEGO. It can be **minifigure scale**, or **microscale**, or something in between. Make it a medieval village or a futuristic settlement. Try to include at least two or three different buildings and a street scene in front of them.

TRY THIS!

- ☐ Include the types of buildings you might see in a village: an inn, a bakery, or a guard tower.
- ☐ Build just the fronts of the buildings so you can see inside them.
- ☐ Bring your village to life with a story.

ILLAIN

Make up your own evil mastermind character and then build their secret base, or their evil vehicle, from LEGO. First decide what powers your villain has and what kinds of things they like. Can they shoot icicles from their fingers, but love tacos? Do they keep pet spiders and can they breathe underwater? Choose some strong colours for your villain; they don't have to be dark colours (hint: choose colours that you have lots of LEGO **parts** in).

TRY THIS!

☐ Every villain has a plan to take over the world. What super-evil machine or weapon will be in the villain's base or vehicle?

☐ Does your villain have henchmen and women? A robot army? Trained underwater spider assassins?

☐ You could even create a superhero to battle your villain.

LEGO Language

Vignette
(noun) *say* vinyet

A small LEGO scene, usually built on an 8x8 base, depicting a single, frozen moment in time that tells a part of a story. Think of it as a still from a movie. For example, a **minifig** artist stands at his easel with a paintbrush in his hand. The background behind him looks like a famous painting of a starry night. Could he be Vincent van Gogh?

VOLCANO

Build a LEGO scene of a volcano. It could be a **microscale** volcano with billowing clouds of smoke rising from it, or a **minifigure-scale** house built next to a lava river. If you have any transparent orange, red or yellow LEGO **parts** you can use them to make the lava look really hot. If you have any LEGO lights (see page 167), you could even use them to make it glow.

TRY THIS!

☐ Check out real volcanoes online for inspiration.
☐ Snake lava across your build to make it look like it's flowing.
☐ Make the lava look red-hot by contrasting the fiery colours with darker-coloured surroundings like grey, black or brown.

PRO TECHNIQUE
VERTICAL

When you're going tall with your LEGO builds, it's important to strengthen your structure. The simplest way to start is to ensure that you're overlapping your LEGO **bricks** as much as possible, making sure each split between **parts** is locked down with another part going across it on top (just like real bricks).

The next thing to think about is reinforcement. One of the best ways to do this is to connect horizontal layers of bricks with long pieces going vertically. You can do this with **SNOT** (see page 258) such as **brackets** or SNOT bricks, but it's important to know your LEGO maths (see page 166) to get them to connect properly. By doing this, you'll make the walls stronger and be able to build taller models.

TALL WALL

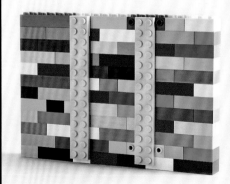

SNOT STRONG

V

W is for...

W

WAND

Your invitation to the school of Witchcraft and Wizardry has arrived! First of all, you'll need a wand, so build one out of LEGO®. It can be anything you like: a slick wooden wand like a certain boy wizard has, or a crazier design that you come up with yourself. It can have sparkly bits, lights, designs and cool colours. Make it look like it's full of magic and ready to turn everyone into a newt.

TRY THIS!

- ☐ You should be able to wave your wand, so make it strong.
- ☐ The end of your wand (where the magic comes out) should have something special: see if you have any translucent or shiny LEGO **parts** you can add.

I have
the power.

W

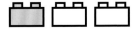

WATCHER

A great optical illusion to try and create is one in which a monster seems to watch you and move its head to follow you around the room. Basically, the way you do it is to make the head inside out — but it looks like it's the right way out from most angles. Perspective tricks your eyes to create the illusion. You'll need to make a large head for the trick to work.

TRY THIS!

☐ Make sure that you balance (see pages 38–39) the weight of the head so the model won't fall over.

LEGO Language

Wedge
(noun) *say* wej

A LEGO block or **plate** that tapers horizontally at one end. These pieces are most commonly used as wings for planes and spaceships, but are also employed when the object needs to be contoured and streamlined. And, if needed, they are a great way to hold a door open.

Wheel
(noun) *say* weel

A circular object that revolves on an axle attached to a vehicle, enabling it to roll easily along the ground. This is true both in the real world and the LEGO world. Except that LEGO wheels are a lot smaller and the tyres don't go flat quite so easily.

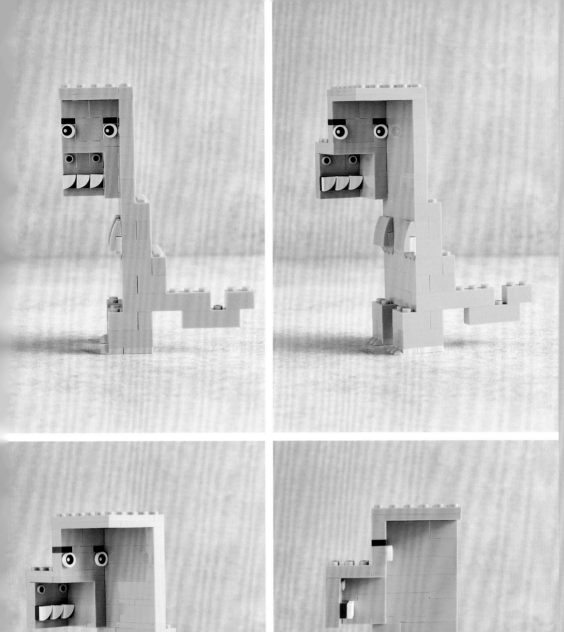

W

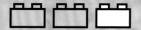

WINGS

Flight is an amazing ability that is shared by only a few creatures: birds, bats and insects can use their wings to soar through the air. Humans have achieved flight too in a number of ways: balloons, planes, helicopters and jet packs. But what about other animals, vehicles and things that don't have wings? Try giving wings to something that doesn't usually fly. How about a blue whale soaring through the air? What would a flying fridge look like? What kind of wings would lift a house?

TRY THIS!

- [ ] Make the wings look like they belong, or make them totally crazy!
- [ ] Create a scene with your flying creature or object: how would you react if you saw it flying towards you?

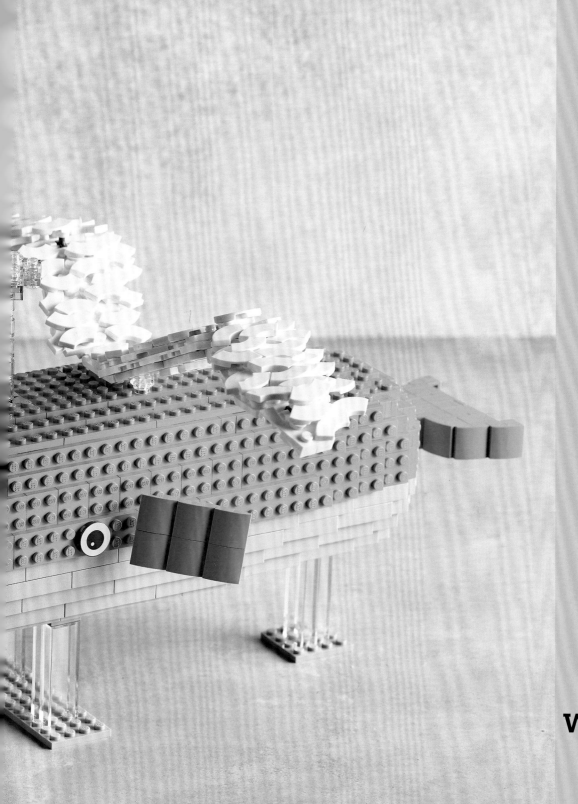

W

303

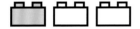

WONDERS

There are lots of cool and amazing places around the world that you can use as inspiration. Look up a country you don't know much about, find out about its wonders, landmarks and buildings and then have a go at building one of them. They can be any scale you like: **microscale**, **minifigure scale** … but maybe not life-size.

TRY THIS!

- ☐ The wonder you create could be anything the place is famous for: a type of food, an animal or a person.
- ☐ Build the flag of the country the wonder is from, or use **SNOT lettering** to make the name of the country.

LEGO Language

Wig
(noun) *say wig*

These are the bare facts: every LEGO **minifigure** is bald. The head **parts** rarely have hair moulded on them, so we have to give them special little hairpieces. Funnily enough, some hair-brained person decided these hairpieces should be called wigs. The long and short of it is that there are many different colours and styles available, but that's just all off the top of my head.

W

PRO TECHNIQUE
WATER

One of the more difficult things to replicate with LEGO is water and other liquids. But it's really worth trying. You can make puddles with **tiles** of different shapes. If you have enough transparent tiles, you can layer them on top of various blues to make quite convincing seas and oceans. And there are plenty of detail **parts** to make splashes and waterspouts. Try making a fountain, a pool, a river, an ocean or any other kind of water you can think of. Then you can move on to other liquids, such as a lake of orange juice!

SEA FOAM

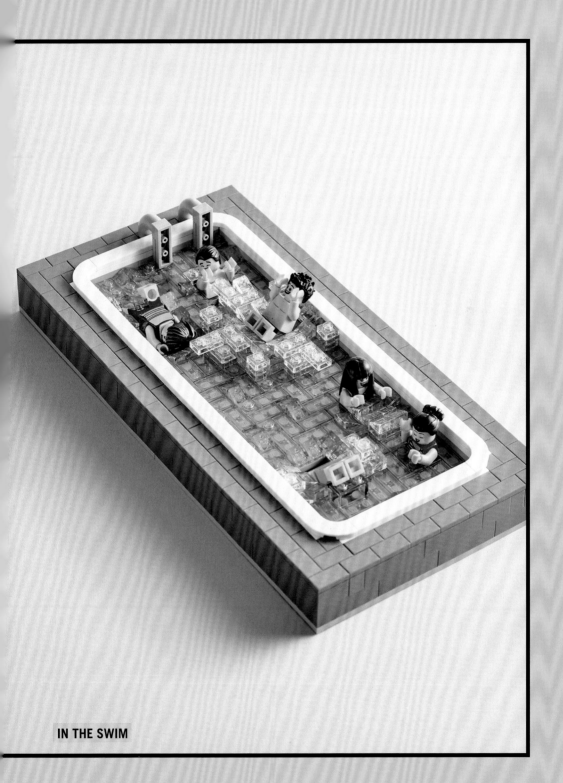

IN THE SWIM

X is for...

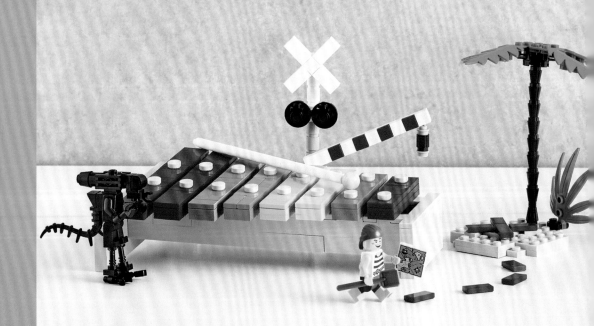

X

X MARKS THE SPOT

Build a LEGO® treasure map. Take either a **baseplate** or a big **plate** and make a map (see pages 172–173) of somewhere you know, like your house or a local park. Think about where you want to hide your treasure in real life and mark it on the map with an X. Then challenge your family and friends to use your map to find the treasure. You could even make the treasure itself out of LEGO. But remember, if you're going to bury it, make sure it's in a plastic bag or box to protect it from the dirt.

TRY THIS!

- ☐ Add a compass or arrow pointing north so people know how to hold the map.
- ☐ Make the landmarks recognisable so that other people can follow your map.

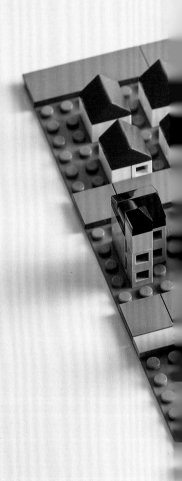

X-RAY

X-rays let you see inside things that are solid. Make a skeleton of a person or animal in a light colour on a dark **plate** or background. This is another opportunity for some **N.P.U.** as you look for LEGO **parts** and **minifig accessories** that you can use to represent the different bones. Or you could build a cutaway LEGO model where you can see the outside on one side and the inside on the other; it could be a shark, a house or an everyday object.

TRY THIS!

☐ Do some research before you start this one: find some X-rays or pictures of skeletons of creatures, or diagrams of machines, and use them to guide your build.

☐ If you're creating an X-ray of a house or building, add some fun hidden secrets, such as buried treasure or a magic portal.

LEGO Language

X-Pod
(noun) *say* eks-pod

X-Pods were a range of LEGO sets released between 2004 and 2006, in which the parts were packaged inside LEGO pods. These pods featured <u>dish</u>-like parts on the top and bottom that included <u>studs</u> and <u>anti-studs</u> to allow them, and the pods themselves, to be attached to regular LEGO models.

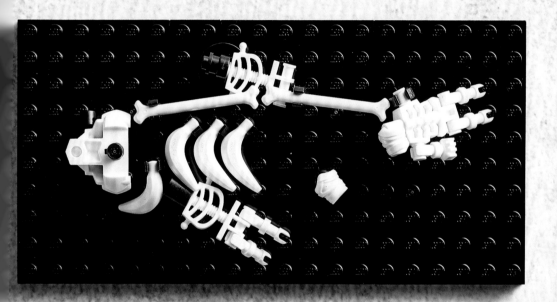

Bone up on skeletons.

X

XYLOPHONE

Build a xylophone from LEGO **bricks**. Try to make each bar a different colour to form a rainbow or pattern. Add it to your collection of LEGO musical instruments (see page 178).

TRY THIS!

- ☐ Your xylophone doesn't have to be life-size: make it as small (or large) as you need to.
- ☐ Don't forget to make a mallet to play your xylophone with.
- ☐ Make a xylophonist to play the instrument.

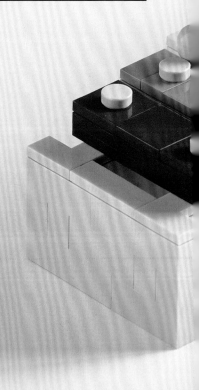

e**X**HAUSTED

Build a bed or a comfortable place to relax for your favourite LEGO **minifig**. Make sure it suits the minifig's character, and is cosy and relaxing so that they can get some well-earned rest.

TRY THIS!

- [ ] Start by building your minifig: the more interesting the character, the better!
- [ ] What sort of things would they do to relax?
- [ ] Get a friend or family member to design the minifig, for more of a challenge.

FI

Do you have something lying around the house that's broken or has a missing part? Why not try to fix it with LEGO? If what's missing or broken has a matching part that's still attached, make your LEGO replacement to match it. It could be a new drawer handle, a picture frame or the lid of a box. Maybe your LEGO replacement will be even better than the original.

TRY THIS!

- [ ] Start with what USED to be there, and try to recreate it with LEGO.
- [ ] If what you're fixing gets used a lot, make the new piece strong and secure.

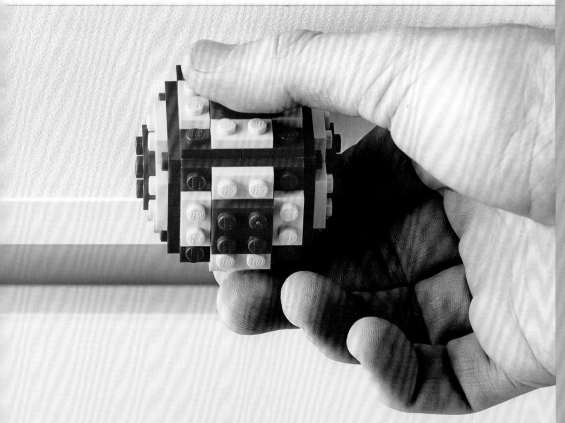

PRO TECHNIQUE
EXTINCT

Just as new LEGO **parts** are created all the time, there are some old LEGO parts and colours that are no longer made, many of which can be really useful. The most obvious eXtinct LEGO parts are in old versions of colours: LEGO's brown, light grey and dark grey parts all used to be much more muted, slightly yellower versions of the colours that are produced now (see **Bley**, page 30). Mixing these old parts with the new colours can create a much more natural, weathered appearance. Some old versions of parts actually allow types of **connections** that new parts do not. Look out for these older parts at second-hand stores to make your LEGO builds more versatile.

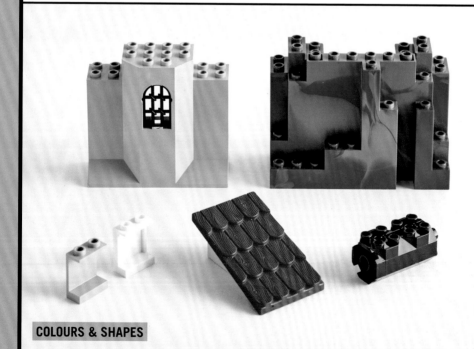

FINGER HINGES

GEARS & AXLES

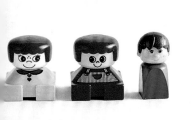

PEOPLE

MINIFIG ANCESTORS

WHAT COULD YOU MAKE WITH THESE EXTINCT PARTS?

X

Y is for...

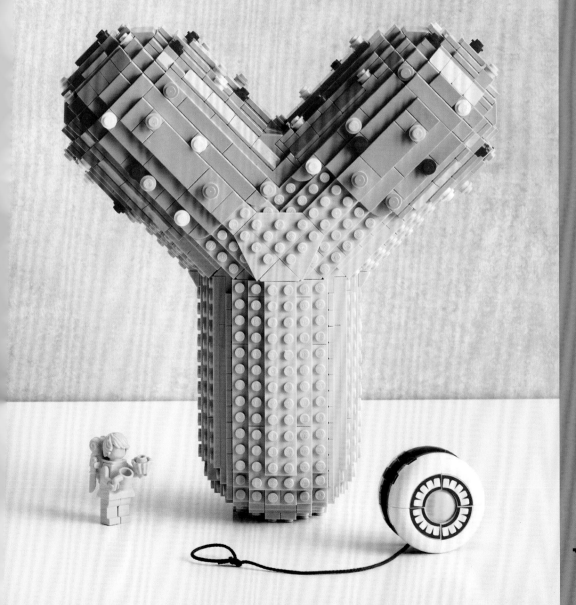

YELLOW

Did you know that the most common LEGO® colour is yellow? **Minifigures** are yellow, basic **bricks** are yellow, and yellow has the greatest number of different pieces. Pick out the colour that you have the most of (it might be yellow) and make something with just those **parts**. It doesn't have to be something that is normally that colour, though: what would the Eiffel Tower look like if it was yellow?

TRY THIS!

- ☐ Remember, it doesn't have to be yellow: just use a colour you have the most of.
- ☐ Focus on getting the shape right because the colour doesn't matter.
- ☐ Did you know LEGO now makes parts in three different shades of yellow?

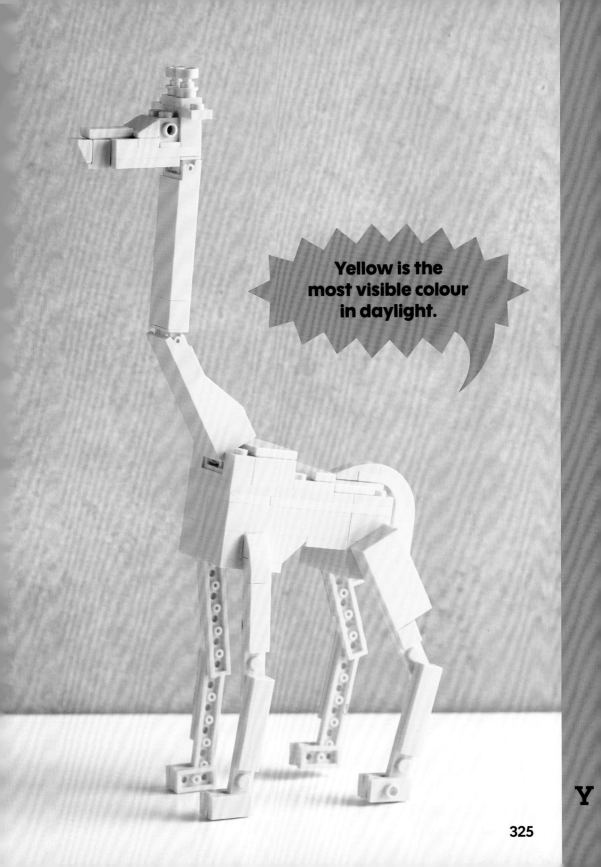

Yellow is the
most visible colour
in daylight.

Y

YUCKY

Build something yucky! It could look like gross radioactive slime with gooey mutant eyeballs, or a slobbery monster with boogers that lives in a rubbish bin. Perhaps it's something you left under your bed that now has its own ecosystem, or a forgotten sandwich in the bottom of your bag that's turned into a science experiment. Make it as repulsive as you can and use colours that remind you of icky stuff.

TRY THIS!

- ☐ Making things look messy or yucky with LEGO can be hard! Try using **clips** and **bars** to twist **connections** off grid and attach more organic LEGO **parts** to simulate tentacles or ooze.
- ☐ Green colours like olive and lime are good for slime and mould.
- ☐ Add some scared or disgusted **minifigs** to your yucky scene.

LEGO Language

Yellowing
(adjective) *say yelohwing*

LEGO is made from ABS plastic, which degrades when exposed to the UV rays in sunlight. If LEGO has been left in the sun for a long time, parts begin to turn slightly yellow.

YFOL
(noun) *say wuy-fol*

An acronym for Young Fan Of LEGO. *See also* **AFOL** and **KFOL** .

#

Think of something you love to eat – it could be cake, an ice-cream sundae, spaghetti and meatballs, a hamburger with salad and cheese, a caramel thickshake, or any meal that you love. Now build that yummy thing, using colours as close to the actual food as you possibly can. Add details and decorative pieces to show ingredients and flavour, and build a plate, bowl or container to display the food and add to its attraction. Don't forget some dipping sauce.

TRY THIS!

- ☐ Use LEGO <u>tiles</u> to add contrasting texture to your food build.
- ☐ Make a knife and fork or a spoon or chopsticks to eat your delicious LEGO meal.
- ☐ For an extra challenge (or if you don't have all the right coloured <u>parts</u>), make the food out of parts in just one colour.

YOUR MUM'S LEGO SET

When you're stuck for inspiration, you may not need to look for something new to build, but instead look to old builds that you could give a new lease of life to. Maybe it's an actual LEGO set that you really enjoyed years ago when you were younger, or something you created yourself but had to compromise on at the time due to a lack of pieces. Going back to old models and redesigning them with new pieces and techniques will bring some fun challenges and problems to solve, but without the initial brainstorming phase.

MUCH MORE MODERN

Z is for...

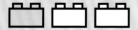

ZEBRA

Zebras are distinctive for their contrasting coats of black and white. Create a LEGO® model of anything you like, but build it in just two contrasting colours, such as black and white, red and blue, yellow and magenta, or any contrasting colours you like.

TRY THIS!

☐ You can start by building something that is often striped in real life, such as a zebra or a cat.

☐ For a harder challenge, try building something that isn't normally stripy … with stripes.

Am I white with black stripes or black with white stripes?

Z

ZODIAC

The practice of telling people's fortunes using astrology has been around for thousands of years. Human beings are captivated by the stars, both as emblems of fate and wonder, and in the science of modern-day astronomy. What star sign were you born under? Use this as inspiration for a model: you could build the creature or thing that represents your star sign (say, a crab for Cancer or a bull for Taurus) or you could build a map of the constellation itself. You don't need to believe in astrology to enjoy the mythology of the zodiacal stars, and they make great subject matter.

TRY THIS!

☐ Did you know that zodiac signs are also grouped into the four elements: Earth, Air, Fire and Water? Use the element of your star sign to inspire the decorations on your model.

LEGO Language

Znap
(noun) *say* znap

Znap was the name of a short-lived LEGO theme from 1998 that was intended as a kind of simpler version of the **Technic**™ system: it had large ready-made beam sections that slotted together with universal joining pieces.

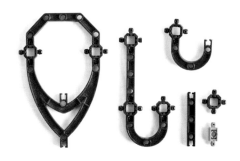

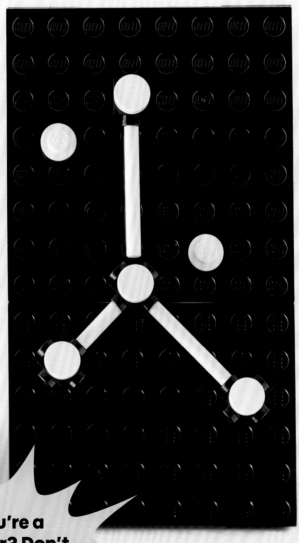

You're a Cancer? Don't get crabby with me.

Z

Zoo

What's your favourite animal? Build a
LEGO zoo enclosure for them. Do some
research first: make sure you know all
about where your animal likes to live. Do
they like a hot or cold climate? Do they live
in a rainforest or underwater? Include their
favourite food, shelter for them to sleep
in, plus somewhere for them to play and
somewhere for **minifig** zoo visitors to stand
and watch them.

TRY THIS!

- Don't forget to add plants to simulate
  your creature's natural habitat.
- Build lots of animal enclosures and clip
  them together to create a mini zoo for
  your minifigures to visit.

Who's who
in the zoo?

PRO TECHNIQUE
ZOOM

Something that's tricky to show in a static LEGO model is movement, especially fast movement. Here we can take a leaf out of the comic book's book. When you want to indicate movement, such as a car zooming along, you can use the same little motion lines that are used in comic books to show direction and speed ... like little trails behind the object. Because LEGO tends towards the cartoony, you can get away with cartoon effects like this. It can also aid the viewer in 'reading' the scene and seeing the action a little better, and so helps to tell your story more effectively.

AIR SWOOSHING

LEGO SLIPSTREAM

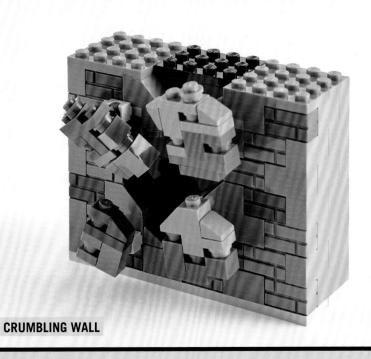
CRUMBLING WALL

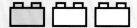

A-Z

This book is an A to Z of ideas, techniques and terms, all to do with LEGO. Now you're here at the end of the book, it's time to make your own alphabet of things that mean something to you. Look at each letter and decide what's the most important or fun thing that starts with that letter. Your alphabet will be different from everyone else's, so display it with pride. Play well!

TRY THIS!

- ☐ Open the book at a random page and try the Design Challenge.
- ☐ Choose the first letter of your name and build everything in that chapter.

Colour Guide

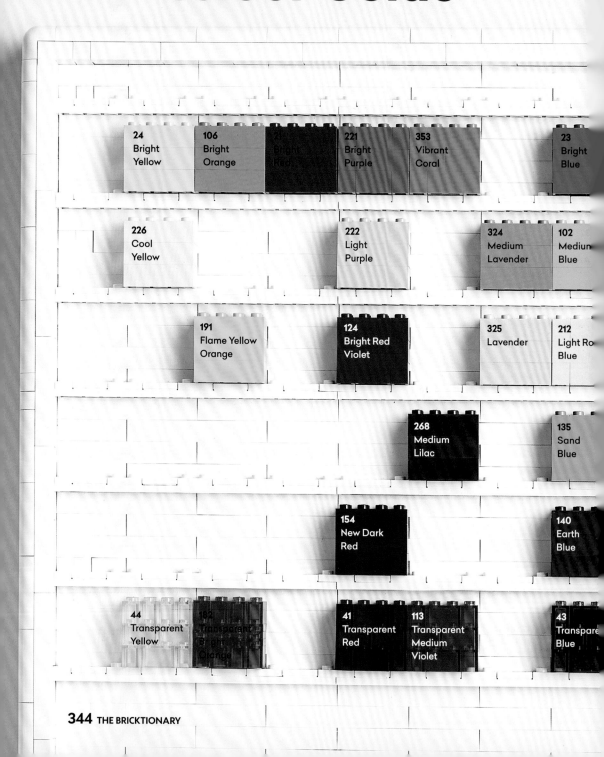

24 Bright Yellow

106 Bright Orange

21? Bright Red

221 Bright Purple

353 Vibrant Coral

23 Bright Blue

226 Cool Yellow

222 Light Purple

324 Medium Lavender

102 Medium Blue

191 Flame Yellow Orange

124 Bright Red Violet

325 Lavender

212 Light Ro. Blue

268 Medium Lilac

135 Sand Blue

154 New Dark Red

140 Earth Blue

44 Transparent Yellow

182 Transparent Bright Orange

41 Transparent Red

113 Transparent Medium Violet

43 Transpare Blue

LEGO® has a set of standard colours for its bricks that rarely changes, though it sometimes adds new colours or retires old ones. These are LEGO's official colour names, though some fans have their own names for certain colours.

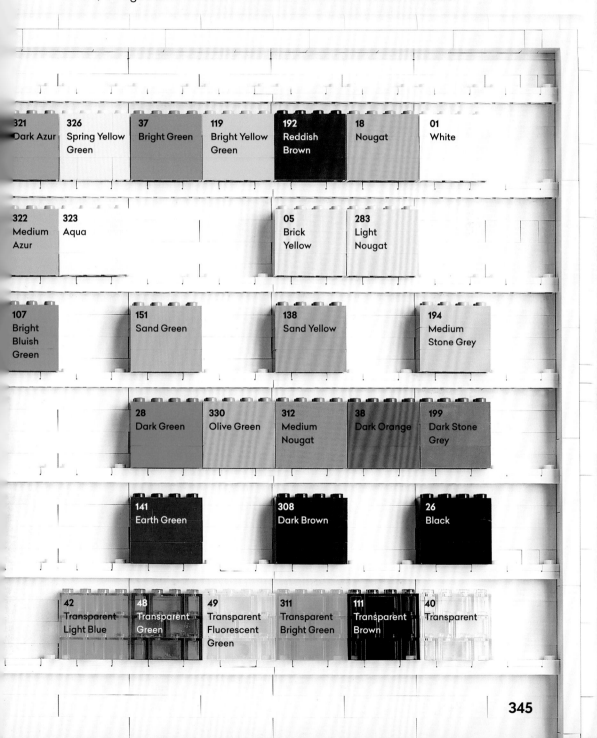

321 Dark Azur	326 Spring Yellow Green	37 Bright Green	119 Bright Yellow Green	192 Reddish Brown	18 Nougat	01 White
322 Medium Azur	323 Aqua			05 Brick Yellow	283 Light Nougat	
107 Bright Bluish Green	151 Sand Green		138 Sand Yellow		194 Medium Stone Grey	
	28 Dark Green	330 Olive Green	312 Medium Nougat	38 Dark Orange	199 Dark Stone Grey	
	141 Earth Green		308 Dark Brown		26 Black	
42 Transparent Light Blue	48 Transparent Green	49 Transparent Fluorescent Green	311 Transparent Bright Green	111 Transparent Brown	40 Transparent	

Design Challenges

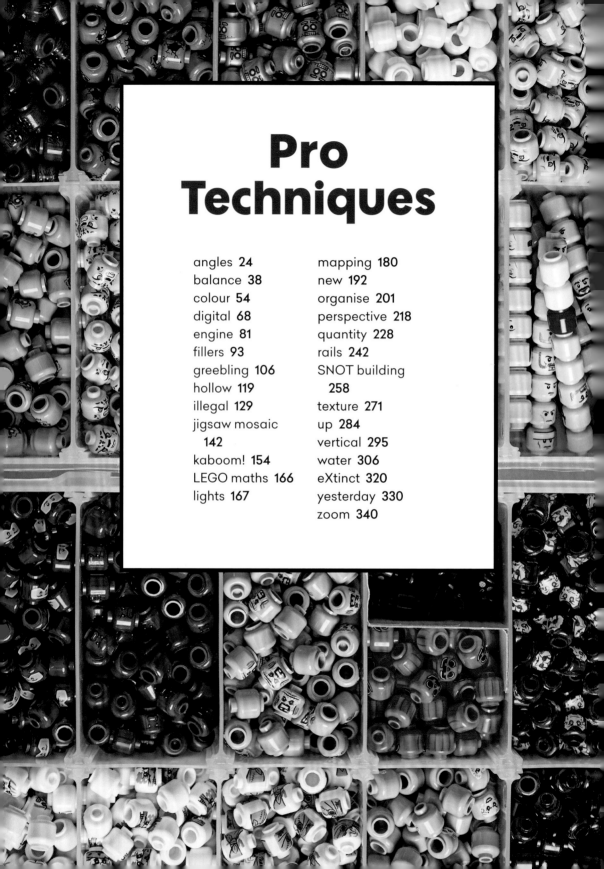

Pro
Techniques

LEGO® GUESSING GAME ANSWERS

Did you spot all of these on the opening page for each letter?

A Accordion, Adventurer, Alien abduction, Alligator, **Alpine**, Ambulance, Ant, Apple, Archaeologist, Archer, Arrows, Athlete, Avalanche

B Bagpipes, Balancing, Balloon, Banana, Banjo, Bats, Bear, Bed, Beekeeper, Bees, Bicycles, Birds, Birthday, Boat, **Book**, Bunny, Burger, Bus, Butterflies

C Cactus, Camel, Campfire, Car, Carrot, Cash, Cat, Centaur, Centurion, Cereal, Cheerleader, Cherries, Chicken, Clam, **Cliff**, Climber, Clock, Clown, Construction worker, Corn, Cornflakes, Costumes, Cow, Cowboy, Crabs, Criminal, Crocodile, Crowbar

D Dachshund, Daisy, Dalmatian, Death Star, Deckchair, Deinonychus, Devo (the rock band), Diamonds, Digger, Dinosaur, **Disco**, DJ, Doctors, Dogs, Dolphin, Dominos, Donut, Dragon, Drum, Duck, Dynamite

E Ear, Earring, Easel, Easter bunny, Echidna, **Electronics**, Elephant, Elf, Emperor, Emu, Eyeball

F Fan, Fence, Fire engine, Firefighters, Fish, Flag, Flames, Flamingo, Flowers, Fly, Fossil, Fox, French bulldog, French person, Frog, **Future**

G Gecko, **Geography**, Giraffe, Globe, Gold, Gong, Gramophone, Green spaceman, Guitar

H Hair, Hammer, Heart, Highlander, **Hollywood**, Horses

I Ibex, Ice block, Ice cream, Iceskating, Igloo, Iguana, Infant, Ink, Insect, **Instruments**, Irish person, Iron, Island, Ivy

J Jam, Japanese flag, Jellyfish, **Jester**, Jet pack, Judge, Jumping castle

K Kangaroo, Karate, Kayak, Kettle, Key, Keyboard, Kid, King, Kite, Kitten, Knight, **Knitting**, Koala, Kraken

L **Laboratory**, Lake, Lamp, Leaves, LEGO, Lemon, Leprechaun, Liberty, Lightbulb, Lime, Lioness, Llama, Lumberjack

M **Magic**, Magician, Maraca, Melon, Mermaid, Monkeys, Motorcycle, Mouse, Mushroom

N Nails, Necklace, Nest, Net, Newspaper seller, **Night**, Ninja, Noise, Note, Notepad, Nurse, Nut

O Oars, Oboe, Octopus, Olives, Orange, Orangutan, Orca, Organ, Ostrich, **Outdoors**, Oven, Owl

P Park, Pen, Pencils, Penguin, Performer, Piano, **Pink**, Pirate, Plane, Plants, Polar bear, Postbox

Q Quail, Quarter, Quaver, **Queen**, Question mark, Quicksand, Quill, Quince, Quintuplets, Quokka

R Rabbit, Racing car, Racquet, Radar, Railway track, Rain hat, Rat, Rattle, Rhino, Ring, Robber, **Robots**, Rocket, Rooster, Rowing boat

S Sandcastle, Satellite, Saturn, Saxophone, Seagull, Seesaw, Slide, **Space**, Space shuttle, Stars, Starship, Sun, Sunglasses, Swan, Swings, Swordfish

T Table, Tall, Toilet, **Toys**, Traffic light, Treasure, Treasure chest, Tree, Triangle, Trombone, Trophy, Truck, Trumpet, Tyres

U UFO, Ukulele, Umbrella, Undertaker, **Underwater**, Unicorn, Unicycle, Urchin, Ursula (from *The Little Mermaid*)

V Vacuum cleaner, Vampire, Van, Vase, Vegetables, Velociraptor, Vet, **Vines**, Violet, Volcano, Vomit

W Waffle, Walkie-talkie, Walrus, Wand, Wanted poster, Wasp, Watermelon, Welder, Wheelbarrow, Whip, White, **Wild West**, Witch, Wizard, Wombat, Wonder Woman, Wrench

X railway X-ing, X marks the spot, Xenomorph, **X-ray**, X-wing, Xylophone

Y Yacht, Yarn, Yellow, Yolk, Yo-yo, **Yum**

Z Zamboni, Zap, Zebra, Zebra crossing, Zeppelin, Zero, Zigzag, Zipper, **Zombies**, Zucchini

Thanks

Making a second (I still can't believe that we've done another one!) book like this isn't possible without the help of a lot of people, in no particular order:

Mark and Darren. Two of the most creative and passionate LEGO® builders there are: the dedication and commitment you bring comes out in everything you do. This book really tested the depths of everything LEGO we know, and you guys rocked it.

The whole Brickman Team. Our not-so-small team is such an incredible LEGO-building group, so diverse in ideas and imagination. The responsibility to inspire millions of children is not taken lightly, and it shows.

Everybody on the Murdoch Books team – Jacqui, Jane, Mark, Megan, Melody and Virginia – made making this second book as easy as the first!

Thank you to LEGO for making the most amazing thing in the form of little plastic bricks. Never in my wildest dreams would I have imagined that your bricks would influence me the way they have. The ability to create and inspire the builders of tomorrow is a unique opportunity and I'm so very thankful.

To Helene, Tormod, Claus, Angie and Leah, thank you for all of your support from the LEGO group.

Thanks also to Mum and Nana, for getting me into LEGO all those years ago.

Finally to Hamish and everyone behind *LEGO Masters Australia*, and of course everyone who watches it, thanks for supporting us and keeping the journey going.

RYAN M^cNAUGHT

Flames, Ice Crystals,
Star Wands, Flame
TM, Dragon's Fire

Flags, Indian Feather,
Bandana, Feather

Insects - Snakes,
Scorpions, Spiders, Bats,
Rats

Animals - Owls, Chickens,
Parrots, Birds

Candles, Lamps,
Assembly Element,
Printed Timber Tiles

Medical, Cameras,
Magnifying Glass,
Binoculars

Mini Figure Trophy

Micro Figure &
Norbet

Food - Ice cream

Food - Apple,
Carrots, Ch

STARWARS
MINIFIGS

READY MADE
MINIFIGS

Published in 2022 by Murdoch Books, an imprint of Allen & Unwin

Murdoch Books Australia
Alexander Street
Crows Nest NSW 2065
Phone: +61 (0)2 8425 0100
murdochbooks.com.au
info@murdochbooks.com.au

Murdoch Books UK
Ormond House
26–27 Boswell Street
London WC1N 3JZ
Phone: +44 (0) 20 8785 5995
murdochbooks.co.uk
info@murdochbooks.co.uk

For corporate orders and custom publishing,
contact our business development team at
salesenquiries@murdochbooks.com.au

Publisher: Jane Morrow
Editorial Manager: Virginia Birch
Creative Direction and Design: Northwood Green
Editor: Melody Lord
Photographer: Mark Roper, except pages 8-9, 112
  and 201 by Armelle Habib
Prop Stylist: Lee Blaylock
Production Director: Lou Playfair

*We acknowledge that we meet and work on the
traditional lands of the Cammeraygal people
of the Eora Nation and pay our respects to their
elders past, present and future.*

ISBN 978 1 92235 180 7 Australia
ISBN 978 1 91166 844 2 UK

 A catalogue record for this
book is available from the
National Library of Australia

A catalogue record for this book is available
from the British Library

Colour reproduction by Splitting Image Colour
Studio Pty Ltd, Clayton, Victoria

Printed by C&C Offset Printing Co., Ltd, China

10 9 8 7 6 5 4 3 2 1

MIX
Paper from
responsible sources
FSC® C008047

**This book is for
Tracy, Riley and Alex**

THE
BRICKTIONARY
The ultimate LEGO® A–Z

RYAN McNAUGHT

LEGO Certified
Professional